CORPORATE IDENTITY
DESIGN

CORPORATE IDENTITY
DESIGN

VERONICA NAPOLES

 VAN NOSTRAND REINHOLD
New York

Library of Congress Catalog Card Number 87-6190
ISBN 0-442-26844-0

I(T)P   Van Nostrand Reinhold is an International Thomson Publishing company.
         ITP logo is a trademark under license.

Printed in the United States of America
Designed by Sharen DuGoff Egana

Van Nostrand Reinhold
115 Fifth Avenue
New York, NY 10003

International Thomson Publishing GmbH
Königswinterer Str. 418
53227 Bonn
Germany

International Thomson Publishing
Berkshire House,168-173
High Holborn, London WC1V 7AA
England

International Thomson Publishing Asia
221 Henderson Bldg. #05-1
Singapore 0315

Thomas Nelson Australia
102 Dodds Street
South Melbourne 3205
Victoria, Australia

International Thomson Publishing Japan
Kyowa Building, 3F
2-2-1 Hirakawacho
Chiyoda-Ku, Tokyo 102
Japan

Nelson Canada
1120 Birchmount Road
Scarborough, Ontario
M1K 5G4, Canada

16 15 14 13 12 11 10 9 8 7 6 5

Library of Congress Cataloging-in-Publication Data

Napoles, Veronica, 1951-
    Corporate identity design.
    Bibliography: p.
    Includes index.
    1. Corporate image. 2. Industrial design coordination. 3. Trademarks.
4. Logotype. I. Title.
HD59.2.N36   1988   659.2'85   87-6190
ISBN 0-442-26844-0

To my husband, Michael, for his encouragement and support,
without which completion of this book would not have been possible

CONTENTS

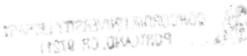

ACKNOWLEDGMENTS

I wish to thank the following people for their valuable contributions to this book: Julie Smith, who helped organize the material and edit the final copy; Walter Landor, for his inspiration and dedication to the profession; Florencio and Elena Napoles, for their unwavering support; Stanley and Sylvia Kleeman, for their enthusiastic and loving concern; my clients, who temporarily took a back seat during the production of the book; my students, who continually serve as an inspiration and reinforced the need for a process-oriented text.

PREFACE

Communication on a symbolic level has been a source of fascination for me since childhood. As an adult, I have learned to apply this fascination, along with experience, to the development of symbolic resources for organizations.

I firmly believe that symbols, in addition to being tools for the marketplace, play an important role for mankind as a universal method of communication and comprehension—a visual language.

When I first started teaching a corporate identity design class, my students encouraged me to write a book based on my lectures and course content. They had expressed a need for a text that was process oriented, not merely a book that consisted of a compendium of symbols.

I tried to stay away from creating a "pretty picture book" and dealt instead with the step-by-step process with which the graphic designer defines, conceptualizes, and implements a corporate identity program. The information in this book can be used for an individual as well as a multidivisional corporation. The book explores the proper meanings of and the differences between the concepts of image and identity, the characteristics of each, the importance and benefit of a corporate identity program, ways of recognizing and dealing with identity problems, and how to conduct a Phase I Creative Exploration—how to generate ideas and how to apply and implement the corporate trademark. Included are a sample proposal and questionnaire, as well as information on how to register trademarks.

I have used *he* throughout the book when referring to either the design consultant or management. This by no means indicates that all designers or managers are male. In writing the book, this was something over which I labored at length. I finally came to the conclusion that using *he* consistently would be grammatically smoother than alternating between *he* and *she* throughout the chapters.

INTRODUCTION TO CORPORATE IDENTITY

The profession of identity designer is a relatively young one, emerging as an independent discipline only in the last forty years. Symbols, however, have been around since the beginning of mankind, over thirty thousand years ago, when man chiseled his first marks onto rock and painted pictures on cave walls in Altamira, Spain. Early man recorded things that he saw or encountered in his everyday life by painting these picture symbols.

Today the role of the symbol has become increasingly important, and its presence is almost limitless in our everyday lives. Everywhere we go, we come across symbols that communicate messages without the use of words. Street signs, restaurants, hotels, airports—all use symbols that communicate to people, regardless of whether or not they speak the same language (fig. 1-1).

It is difficult to trace the exact beginning of corporate identity. Merchant trade symbols from nineteenth-century Europe were prototypes of modern identity design. The symbols were used by crafts and tradespeople alike to identify themselves, their merchandise, or the services they offered (fig. 1-2). These visual identifiers appeared on everything from envelopes to storefronts. In the American West at

the beginning of the century, branding marks were commonly used to identify ownership (fig. 1-3). But the profession of identity design did not become a "legitimate" profession until businesspeople understood the connection between good design and increased sales. The evolution of the profession coincided with the Great Depression of the 1930s. Most companies at that time were wringing their hands nervously, playing a wait-and-see game. Many of the business groups that were to become important in the next decades seized the initiative and launched newly designed products, with distinctively superior marketing strategies. Some of the "trade characters" that emerged at this time were the Dutch boy, Elsie the Borden cow, the RCA audiophile dog, Buster Brown and his dog Tiger, the Smith Brothers (Trade and Mark), and Mobil's Pegasus (fig. 1-4). Artists were commissioned during this time to work on corporate identities, but they were often far removed from the corporate decision makers and the consumer environment in which the product or service was to exist. Very few designers in the early days of the profession dealt directly with top-level management.

In the late 1930s, the clean lines of the Bau-

1-1. Symbols used in transportation-related facilities as developed by the American Institute of Graphic Arts for the Department of Transportation.

1-2. In nineteenth-century Europe, merchant trade symbols were prototypes of modern identity design. The symbols were used by crafts and tradespeople alike to identify themselves, their merchandise, or services offered. From left to right: trade symbols for carpenter, tailor, and horseshoer.

1-3. *In the American West at the beginning of the century, branding marks were commonly used to identify ownership.*

1-4. Top row: *Elsie the Borden cow, designed by Gianninoto Associates, the RCA (Radio Corporation of America) dog. Bottom row: the Mobil Oil Pegasus and Buster Brown.*

haus school began to influence the face of the printed page, packaging, vehicles, and all corporate communications. Trains, fashion styles, even toasters were given a streamlined look. An attempt was made to have trademarks capture the spirit of these new streamlined products (fig. 1-5).

The true growth of the industrial design profession came during the postwar period, as more trained people entered the field from top-level schools that had started to teach the subject. Raymond Loewy, a French immigrant, turned out the International Harvester mark; Paul Rand designed the IBM mark; and Morton Goldsholl designed the Motorola "M" (fig. 1-6). This period marked a turning point in the profession. Until this time, graphics had been used primarily as decoration. There had been no recognition of the correlation between design and success in the marketplace. Designers now set out to sell businesspeople on design as a marketing and sales tool.

During the 1950s and 1960s, the growth of multinational corporations and the increase of corporate mergers contributed to the redesigning of trademarks that had stood for one product or service. Many of the Fortune 500 companies exchanged their old trademarks for new ones, believing that these would better express the size and scope of their businesses. Elsie the Borden cow and her brood were sent out to pasture; Mobil's Pegasus and a slew of other "trade characters" were retired from service. Companies, however, had to be very careful about "early retirement," as was dem-

1-5. An attempt was made to have trademarks capture the spirit of these new streamlined products. This logo was done in the 1930s for Coffee Sales Company, in Cedar Rapids, Iowa.

1-6. International Harvester mark, designed by Raymond Loewy, the Motorola mark designed by Morton Goldsholl, and IBM, designed by Paul Rand.

1-7. Chermayeff & Geismar designed the abstract Chase Manhattan Bank symbol.

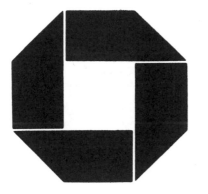

onstrated in 1958 when R. J. Reynolds decided to change the look of the Camel cigarette package by removing two of the three pyramids and modernizing the design. After the first phase had been completed (the removal of one pyramid and a change in typeface), sales immediately dropped and there was a deluge of customer complaints. Needless to say, the old design was promptly reinstated.

Design systems during the early and mid-1960s became the "magic concept," since the mood of the times emphasized consistency, sameness, and uniformity. Everything was slick, from wet-look miniskirts to corporate identity manuals, which delineated every possible application for a symbol or logotype. It was at this time that Chermayeff & Geismar designed the abstract Chase Manhattan Bank symbol (fig. 1-7); it was simple and elegant, and it became the model for many other symbols that were to be created during the sixties and beyond.

The 1970s saw a decline in the popularity of corporate symbolism, as most companies were reluctant to admit to spending a million dollars on the launching of a new corporate identity program. After the Watergate scandal and the ensuing social and economic problems, corporations kept a low profile, spending money on social programs, rather than on graphics, to improve their images.

Today designers who are most advanced in their attitudes toward problem solving realize the necessity for an integration of many disciplines in the design process. These capabilities must relate to communications, as well as to aesthetics, and must include behavioral psychology and marketing, as well as the graphic arts. The successful identity designer will be sensitive to all of these disciplines.

Man was a symbol maker long before he was a toolmaker; his desire for identification is deeply embedded in his past. At first, people's names were based on visually distinguishing characteristics, then on occupation, craft, or trade. As individual and cultural activities grew more complex, symbols and methods of identification gradually became more sophisticated. The foundation of the behavioral sciences concerns itself with the study of the outward and visible symbols. It follows then that graphic designers should familiarize themselves with the findings of psychologists and sociologists.

For example, sociologists say that the word "lite," which started as a marketing term for low-calorie products, has infiltrated our lives to the point where "less" is valued above "more." Dr. Clinton Sanders, a sociologist at the University of Connecticut who studies popular culture, says the mobility of American society, both geographically and economically, has helped to bring about a "lite" decade. People can cut calories without changing their diets by using products such as Jell-O Light, Cornitos Light Corn Chips, Real Lite Cola, Lite Steak, Miracle Lite mayonnaise, and then wash it all down with a glass of Christian Brothers Chateau La Salle Light Wine. "Light is a way of thinking that we've come to in the 1980s," says Dr. Robert T. London, a psychiatrist at New York University Medical Center. "It's an umbrella phenomenon where lightness transforms itself into the cars we drive, the lightness in a room, our diet, as well as lightness in the relationships we have." [1]

From a technical standpoint, designers should also be thoroughly familiar with the tools of the trade. All graphic designers must know how to utilize and manipulate the wide range of tools, materials, and resources available, in order to create a language using symbols and typography.

However, before a businessperson or a designer embarks on a corporate identity program, there must be a complete understanding of the two concepts: image and identity.

IMAGE VERSUS IDENTITY

Corporations are like people—they have individual characteristics, cultural impressions, and philosophies. Yet, to the public they often seem "cold" and "characterless"—listless, with no visible signs of life. A trademark, the visible part of the corporate identity program, helps to "humanize" a company by presenting a face, a personality, in the form of a symbol. The symbol reflects the company's *identity* and helps to mold its *image* in a positive way. Understanding the difference between the concepts of corporate image and corporate identity is the first step toward closing the gap between the two.

The corporate image is the way in which a company is perceived by the public—consumers, competitors, suppliers, the government, and the general public. Corporate identity, on the other hand, is a symbol that reflects the way in which the company *wants* to be perceived. It is the ideal situation, and can be *created*; whereas image is always earned.

Corporate image is developed through contact with the company, and by interpreting information about the firm. How is the company currently being perceived? How does the company think it is being perceived? These impressions can be obtained through the company's products, buildings, advertising, and business dealings (even down to minute details, such as the way in which a phone is answered). All of these impressions are collected in the minds of employees, bankers, consumers, the press, government officials, and present and potential stockholders, and are organized into a picture of what the firm is like.

Image is constantly changing. As new information and changing business trends are introduced, the new information is added to or modifies the old impression. This information is also subject to the interpretation of the observer's own value framework. For example, the fact that a company is growing and has expanded its staff from nine to sixty-five employees in two years will tell one person that the company is prospering; to another, this same information might indicate that it is an impersonal organization or that it is growing too fast to handle any new business.

The message a company sends about itself can be misinterpreted, amplified, or, even worse, ignored. Since most corporations send out multiple messages, geared both toward specific audiences and toward the public in general, image mutations are common. A healthy corporate image will exhibit or elicit some, if not all, of the following characteristics or reponses:

1. Strong emotional response. The strength of this response increases in direct proportion to the length of time that a particular image has been in use: the qualities associated with the Mercedes Benz cars or Levi Strauss denims are firmly rooted (fig. 1-8). Well-established images can withstand considerable pressure, and, due to the emotional responses they elicit, they are nurtured and treated lovingly by consumers. Once a positive image is established, it is supported by those inside and outside the company alike. Coca-Cola made the mistake of replacing what had been an old friend to the American consumer by taking away the old Coke and replacing it with a product they called "New Coke." In the eleven weeks that followed the introduction of new Coke—which will now be called "Coke" —the executives were astounded at the intense loyalty the American consumers had to the old formula. The company quickly reinstated the old formula Coke under the name "Coke Classic." Asked whether the company's image will suffer from the experience, Mr. Patton, a marketing official at the Coca-Cola Bottling Company, said, "If people were outraged that Coke took the old formula away, then they have to be grateful we're bringing it back." He added, "It only means our boss is the consumer. I wish we had understood their deep emotions."[2]

2. Appearance of power. Consumers want to feel the power and strength of a corporation through association with its commodities or services. Customers want to feel that they are dealing with an organization that is stable and reliable when they are buying its services or investing in the company.

3. Sense of experience, confidence, and tradition. When a company has established these characteristics, it is able to launch new products based on its past performance. Advertising personnel can use tag lines such as, "New! From the makers of Pepsi-Cola" (fig. 1-9), capitalizing on the established reputation of the company and its products. A company with an established image has a greater advantage over a company without one when it comes to takeover bids, tenders, or environmental issues, as it can stand on its past achievements.

4. Slow process. The image-building process is a slow one; and change is not effective until it is accepted by the observer. A sound image will have been built only after a fairly lengthy period of consistent operations has occurred.

1-8. *The Levi Strauss mark created by Landor and Associates.*

1-9. Companies can introduce new products that ride on the success of previous products. For example, Pepsi-Cola introduced their new product Slice with an endorsement on all promotional material: "NEW! from the makers of Pepsi-Cola."

Corporate identity is the visual counterpart of corporate image. It consists of the symbolic mark that reflects a desired image.

Effective corporate identities, like effective corporate images, have certain common characteristics:

1. Symbolism tends to strengthen simple associations. Simplicity is fundamental to a good brand-package-symbol identification combination. The Mercedes Benz star makes a brief, simple, and unmistakable statement of quality (fig. 1-10).

2. A strong visual trigger. A substantial portion of a symbol's power lies in its ability to trigger a response to a product or company. An entire program is built around the identification symbol. Whenever a member of the public encounters the company, it should be in the same symbolic terms. If a symbol is effective, a consumer need only think of the industry, or product involved, and the company's identifier will come to mind.

3. Identity as a promotional tool. Corporate symbolism is almost exclusively a promotional tool—active rather than passive. Advertising campaigns usually last a season; identity is more permanent and should last twenty years or more. For example, the stagecoach symbol of the Wells Fargo Bank, created twenty years ago, is still being used successfully as the visual keystone of its advertising and promotional campaigns (fig. 1-11, 1-12).

4. The corporate identity must be memorable. The basic difference between a success-

1-10. The Mercedes Benz star makes a brief, simple, and unmistakable statement of quality.

1-11. The stagecoach symbol of the Wells Fargo Bank, created over twenty years ago by Landor and Associates.

1-12. Wells Fargo uses its identity successfully for advertising and promotional campaigns.

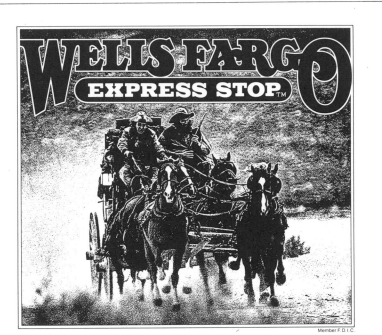

Member F.D.I.C.

<u>Bank at midnight.</u> Or high noon. Wells Fargo now has 24-hour banking. Withdraw cash from your accounts. Make savings or checking deposits. Transfer funds. Check your balances. Make payments on Wells Fargo loans, MasterCard, or Visa.
The Express Stop is the bank that never closes.

Wells Fargo Bank. Since 1852.

ful and unsuccessful corporate identity program is that a successful identification has two important qualities: suggestiveness and recall. When a potential customer wants to buy a product and a particular company's brand name comes to mind, this is *suggestion*. When this same individual comes into contact with the identifier and relates it back to the company it represents, this process is known as *recall*. An effective corporate identification triggers both of these responses without frequent or expensive adjustments.

Sometimes a company's image is not the same as the image it wants to convey; its identity may also be at odds with its image. For a corporation to align the desired identity with its image, it must first recognize that an identity problem exists. Then it must create a suitable identity by implementing a well-conceived program using the kind of step-by-step process that is described in this book. When identity and image are in harmony, the company is perceived as it actually is, as well the way it wants to be perceived by members of its target market. The extent to which identity and image differ indicates the degree of need for a program of realignment.

Corporate identification experts, or "image doctors," as they are sometimes called, have a relationship with their clients that is similar, in a way, to the relationship psychiatrists have with their patients. They help their clients see what they really are—not always a pleasant portrayal.

To illustrate, let us look at a broadcasting company that was losing business. Its executives wanted to appeal to a sophisticated, upper-middle-class audience and believed the station was doing so. When polled, those in top-level management positions said their company had a "Cadillac" image. Yet, a poll of the general public indicated that the station's image was not represented by a Cadillac, but by a beat-up Ford station wagon. To attract the desired listeners and the airtime buyers, the company needed a thorough change of image, all the way from a logo to a new program format.

In a sense, image doctors hold up mirrors so that companies can look at themselves. It takes a lot of courage for companies to look at the way they are seen by the outside world; but seeing what its real image is enables management, through its advertising, public relations, and other kinds of corporate activity, to project itself properly to its various audiences.

2 ESTABLISHING THE NEED FOR A CORPORATE IDENTITY PROGRAM

Even though a firm may have an impressive list of achievements, unless this information reaches the public and its targeted market, it does little good. Management should make an effort to understand its overall image, and should pay as much attention to it as it pays to earnings, policies, and strategic marketing plans. Long-range plans must be made by management that includes corporate identity as an integral part of the total management plan. Changes that affect the success of a company take place not only within, but also outside the company, in its industry and in the world marketplace. An organization must be ready to adapt to these changes. In the battle for corporate survival, organizations that are flexible and that can set new objectives to respond to these changes will endure.

The process of building a successful image is a slow one, rather like changing the direction of an aircraft carrier; although it can take miles for a change to be felt, a wrong turn can mean a serious delay or even disaster.

Many symptoms can signal the need for an identity program.

NAME AND SYMBOL OBSOLESCENCE

A company might be sending out confusing messages about itself or its products. This usually happens when its name or symbol is no longer appropriate.

RCA, for instance, evolved from being a manufacturer of radios into a company active in satellite communications, electronics, and car rentals. When that happened, its familiar symbol visually suggested an inappropriate image for the company (fig. 2-1). The firm undertook an identity program aimed at reflecting its continuing growth and diversification. Robert Sarnoff, then president and chief executive officer (RCA has since been taken over by General Electric), reported " . . . hundreds of approving comments from our customers and competitors, stockholders, and employees. We were especially encouraged by the enthusiastic response of many creative people—product designers, advertising artists, copywriters, and architects—who felt that the new style would liberate and revitalize their efforts to communicate the dynamism and diversity of the company."[3]

2-1. *Old RCA symbol (left), and the new one (right) designed by Lippincott and Margulies.*

CHANGES IN MANAGEMENT

A change in management can sometimes herald the approach of a new identity program. The energy a corporation projects depends in part on the progressive action that is taken by its management. A new chief executive officer can establish his own style of leadership and provide the company with a needed shot in the arm. An identity program could reflect this new vitality.

GROWTH PATTERNS

When a company increases in size, its problems can grow as rapidly as its profits, especially if it has merged with or has been acquired by another firm. Without an identity program that is as much a part of long-term planning as marketing or finance, it could take years before the roles and relationships of the companies really become clear.

Companies usually grow by one of two different strategies, internal or external acquisitions. Companies that develop products internally usually endorse the products by using the corporate signature (for instance, AT&T Computers). Companies that grow through external acquisitions usually maintain the acquired company's name and identification. When Transamerica Corporation acquired Budget Rent-A-Car, the name and graphics remained the same with no visual reference to the parent company. The subsidiary name and graphics were maintained, along with a corporate endorsement.

Communication systems can effectively unify the identification of the subsidiaries and reflect the ideal positioning of each affiliate relative to the corporate parent. Figure 2-2 illustrates the different levels at which companies can be related to one another visually.

LEGISLATIVE IMPACT

In the wake of divestiture and deregulation utilities, once monopolies, are now finding themselves in an increasingly competitive market. In 1983 AT&T was scheduled for divestiture, which would result in seven separate regional telephone companies. Each of these regional companies was independent from the others and from AT&T. The public, generally confused about the split, was soon offered enlightenment in the form of an entire advertising program that explained the new structure, services, and products (fig. 2-3). Each of the new "baby bells"—and AT&T—needed an identity program (fig. 2-4).

LOSS OF EARNINGS

A diminishing profit ratio or an unsatisfactory share of the market is a strong indicator that a company needs to take a long, hard look at itself. Firms that depend on the public to buy their products or services rely heavily on their existing corporate image. The image— whether positive or negative—largely determines the attitudes not only of consumers but of investors, as well as stock analysts and future customers. A good identity program can im-

2-2. *Companies often expand through diversification. The result of this can range from a few operating subsidiaries to a system of subsidiaries numbering in the hundreds. Companies should develop a master identification system showing how the various subsidiaries relate to each other and to the parent corporation. Through the use of an identification system, a subsidiary can be made less or more visible, based upon the benefits to its own operation and/or the corporation. The result is a communication benefit through a coordinated system of company names, trademarks, and other graphic elements, which are achieved through planned identification.*

Level	Signature
Parent	⭐ Enerco
Parent Name with Service Phrase	⭐ Enerco Plastics
Combination of Parent and Subsidiary	⭐ Enerco Duval
Subsidiary with Corporate Linking Phrase	⭐ United Tec An Enerco Company
Subsidiary name and graphics with corporate endorsement	An Enerco Company **VIA**

2-3. *The public, generally confused about the AT&T split, was soon enlightened. An advertising program devoted to explaining the new structure, services, and products was introduced.*

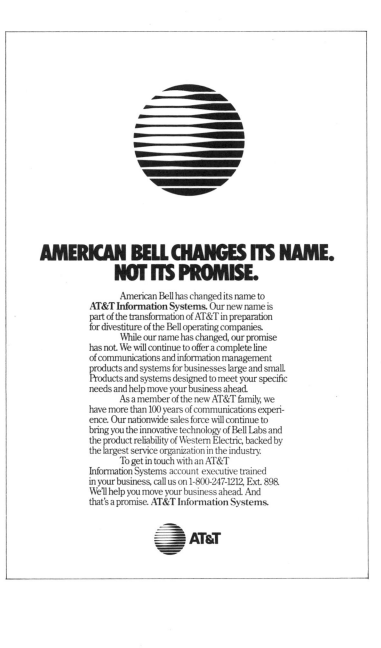

2-4. The divestiture forced each of the newly formed companies to design new logos. (Copyright © 1985 IEEE. Reprinted, with permission, from IEEE SPECTRUM, Vol. 22, No. 11, page 62, Nov. 1985.)

What's in a name?

The familiar blue bell, used to represent the communications industry for almost a hundred years, could have been a Greek cross, a flying figure, or a shield. All three were proposed as symbols to represent the fledgling AT&T long-distance service in 1888. Of course, AT&T chose the blue bell—a basic concept that enjoyed a monopoly of sorts until court agreements gave it to the seven holding companies. After divestiture, AT&T and the seven new companies had to design new logos. Here is how each tackled the problem.

When the Federal Communications Commission called for a fully separate subsidiary to sell Bell-manufactured equipment, AT&T began to develop a new name and logo. Saul Bass/Herb Yeager Associates in Los Angeles, Calif., was commissioned to design a logo symbolizing AT&T's mission to help customers move electronic information around the world. The result was a blue sphere with white striations of varying width and curvature, referred to by AT&T as a "globe or globe symbol." The company then spent $30 million to foster public recognition of the globe. One hundred thousand computer-generated names later, American Bell was chosen as the postdivestiture corporate name for use with the globe symbol. But Federal Judge Harold H. Greene, who had ordered the breakup of the AT&T empire, set aside this choice and directed the company to drop the name Bell.

While doing research for a complying name, Bass/Yeager found that nine out of ten people in the United States associated "AT&T" with financial stability and technological leadership. The result was a marriage between the globe and the name AT&T.

NYNEX

Nynex took the first four letters of its name from the market it was to serve: NY stood for New York, NE for New England. The X originally represented undefined future prospects, but according to a Nynex spokesman, the future of Nynex is bright and the meaning of the X has been changed to represent excellent future prospects. Nynex retained Lippincott & Margulies Inc. of New York City to draft a new logo that did not use the bell seal or name—an omission intended to show that Nynex was a brand-new company that wanted "to make it on its own." To symbolize Nynex's commitment to continue the Bell tradition of quality, Pantone Process Blue, the same blue used for

Charles Whiting   Editorial Intern

AT&T's logo, was kept as the official logo color. The lines flowing from the E through the X were drawn to indicate a forward-looking company in a highly technical age.

BELLSOUTH

The new company comprising the operating companies Southern Bell and South Central Bell settled on using Bell as part of its name in the hope that the public would transfer the image of quality associated with the old Bell System companies to the new corporation. Divestiture agreements required a geographic modifier to be used with Bell, and the new company, which serves the deep South, chose to go with that area in its name. The logo was designed by Burton Campbell Inc. of Atlanta.

Bell Atlantic

Another divested telephone company that kept Bell in its name was the company serving the eastern states of Delaware, Maryland, New Jersey, Pennsylvania, Virginia, West Virginia, and the District of Columbia. To satisfy the constraints imposed by Judge Greene, the company chose Atlantic to describe its area of telephone service. Walter Perkowski, district manager of Bell Atlantic's Corporate Identification Division, designed the logo, complete with "the wave of the future" rolling through the A toward the rest of the word Atlantic. Since divestiture, the wave has rolled across the United States in the form of subsidiary offices.

AMERITECH

American Information Technologies Corp. chose for its new logo and name the word Ameritech. Amer stands, of course, for American and indicates the scope and vision of Ameritech's operation. The I stands for information and represents the movement of information and ideas from place to place—the business of Ameritech. Tech represents a commitment to use the newest and best technology "to give customers superior service at a fair price."

The designer of the logo, Goldsholl Design Inc. of Northfield, Ill., added the sparkle in the A with a dual meaning in mind. First, it represents the explosiveness of the volume of information that can be sent by new transmission technology, and second, it says that Ameritech intends to be a star in the information-transport business. Through all the letters Goldsholl Design drew a line to represent the purest and fastest form of energy—a beam of laser light.

Southwestern Bell Corporation

The Southwestern Bell Corp. elected to keep the Southwestern Bell name and the bell seal it had used while part of the Bell System. "We believe they are extremely valuable business assets," said a company spokesman. "Not only do customers nationwide recognize them, but they also associate them with the qualities we believe our company represents: high quality, dedication to service, and sophisticated technology." The typeface and Bell logo were designed in 1969 by Bass/Yeager Associates in an AT&T corporate-identity project.

PACIFIC TELESIS. Group

Information services often use the asterisk key on the bottom left-hand corner of a telephone keypad as part of the access sequence that allows data retrieval. Pacific Telesis has adopted this symbol, also called the access button, as the centerpiece for its logo. The access button graphically states that the business of the company is information exchange. A red button was chosen because red is a "warm, human color," Pacific Telesis says. And the small lines extending from the asterisk represent a movement toward infinity.

The word Pacific gives the logo a geographic tie to California and Nevada, the two states that make up its service area. According to a Pacific Telesis spokesman, "Telesis is a word that means progress that is intelligently planned and directed." Pacific Telesis can be abbreviated to PacTel, a name familiar to customers who have used it to refer to Pacific Telephone & Telegraph for more than 70 years. PacTel is also the name given to many subsidiaries of Pacific Telephone. Landor Associates of San Francisco designed the logo.

USWEST

US West felt that the spirit of service demonstrated by Mountain Bell, Northwestern Bell, and Pacific Northwest Bell while part of the Bell system had earned it the right to keep the Bell name and seal. The operating companies, however, are regulated, and US West thought these symbols were inappropriate for a holding company comprising both regulated and unregulated subsidiaries. Instead, Hill & Knowlton Inc., the designers, chose US to symbolize the vision of national and international scope for the company and West to capture the spirit of that region—freedom, independence, and control of one's own destiny.

prove profits, increase profit ratio, help a company survive an adverse market, and make financing easier to obtain.

In December 1982, a San Francisco–based savings bank, Hibernia, was sold to First Pacific Group, a Hong Kong multinational firm. First Pacific quickly launched a campaign to grab a share of the upscale banking market by taking two steps—they introduced a new money market account that paid two points more than other banks paid, and they underwent a complete identity change. After a short period of two months, Hibernia Bank chairman Carl D. Gustavson reported eight thousand new affluent customers, and $450 million in new deposits.

The firm's million-dollar campaign changed Hibernia's image from a sleepy community savings bank to an international commercial lender. Gustavson explained the move succinctly: "We're buying a share of the market."[4]

COMPANIES ABOUT TO BE SOLD

If ticketed for divestiture, companies will sometimes undergo a face-lift and put on a new dress before being put on the auction block. Under the Margaret Thatcher government, the British are converting state-owned enterprises into private firms. One of these firms, British Airways, was slated for divestiture and wanted to revamp its nondescript image before being sold. British Airways did indeed revamp its look in accordance with a new company strategy befitting a for-profit enterprise (fig. 2-5).

BENEFITS OF A CORPORATE IDENTITY PROGRAM

A favorable corporate image is a just reward in and of itself, since it is one of the most important assets a business can have. In addition, the following are a number of specific benefits that can be earned through a good corporate identity program.

EFFECTS ON ORGANIZATIONAL THINKING

Concerned with profits and the daily grind, executives can sometimes lose touch with the basic questions of corporate purpose by putting corporate planning aside. One of the most valuable functions of an identity program is its catalytic effect on organizational thinking. The program usually provides a platform for dealing with essential questions, such as how the company wants to be perceived and how it will achieve its goals. Through a commitment to a corporate identity program, these issues are dealt with promptly, instead of being pushed aside. The program wakes people up, stimulates ideas, and satisfies the need for executives to participate in corporate direction and planning. Conflicts and differences of opinion are brought out into the open and, as a

2-5. *British Airways revamped its look in accordance with a new company strategy befitting for-profit enterprise.*

result of the program, a new unity of thinking and purpose can be established.

CREAM OF THE CROP

Everyone likes to be on the winning team. People do not want to be part of companies that are losing money or that are looked upon unfavorably by the public. On the other side of the coin, a company is only as good as the people that work for it. Companies with a good corporate image can enlist talented people, actually providing for them the same feeling they might have belonging to an exclusive club. Productivity levels are likely to increase with the increased morale. A secretary who is psychologically committed to the company will be a better, more productive employee and, chances are, a goodwill ambassador for the firm outside the company.

GOOD NETWORKS

Distributors and dealers also want to capitalize on a company whose products or services have a positive image in the minds of prospective customers. A company's products may even be put in a better position on the shelf; the association with a widely accepted product is sought after not only by the consumer, but by the distributor as well.

Establishing a good rapport with suppliers is much easier if the company has a positive image. This can be an invaluable association during times of material shortages. Companies can also receive information from suppliers regarding new materials, competitor activities, and consumer attitudes. Companies can be assured of prompt delivery of goods and a relationship that can have the advantage of attracting new business simply by word of mouth.

IDENTIFICATION OF AUDIENCES

Since most companies send multiple messages about themselves geared toward specific audiences and the public in general, distortions of the image seem to be a constant hazard. With a positive image that minimizes ambiguity, the true character of the company is communicated loud and clear to exactly the right group.

Audiences can take the shape of one or more of the following: stock analysts, stockholders, customers (present, past, and future), suppliers, competitors, present and future employees, government, legislators, and the public in general. Early in the image-building process, management should decide which of these various target audiences are the priorities, as this can affect the process of creating an identity.

NAME FAMILIARITY

Companies with established images have the luxury of introducing new products, services, or concepts into the market more quickly and effectively because of their track records. The customer is more than likely to believe that the products are of better quality, will pay more for the products, and will often buy the new products based on past experience.

RESTORATION OF PUBLIC CONFIDENCE

During the last several years, there has been considerable publicity regarding such controversial issues as environmental pollution, false advertising, poor products, and manufacturers who do not stand behind their guarantees.

Efforts to communicate corporate accomplishments and contributions generate and reinforce a favorable image. Furthermore, companies can establish programs that will reach many people. Providing public-interest films and exhibits that focus on community problems helps to maintain open and extensive communications with the public (fig. 2-6).

A favorable impression will go a long way toward correcting trouble-causing image faults.

2-6. *Companies can establish programs that will reach many people and work on community problems in an attempt to maintain open and extensive communications with the public.*

If we get rid of our basic industries, it'll be just like the good old days.

This is a plug for the farmer. The forester. The aluminum worker. For those 1,000,000 Northwesterners who make a living by actually making something. Theirs are the critical jobs. The jobs that support other jobs—two to one. The day we think we can live without them, is the day we'll have trouble living at all.

The People of the Northwest Aluminum Industry

If the Northwest becomes a service economy, 1,000,000 parents could spend a lot more time with the kids.

All jobs are important. But those in basic industry are critical to this region's future. Every farmer, forester, fisherman and aluminum worker who's employed creates the need for at least two other jobs in the Northwest. Basic industry in this part of the world is just that. Basic.

The People of the Northwest Aluminum Industry

3 WHERE TO BEGIN

Awareness of an existing identity problem is usually the first step toward achieving effective corporate image communication. The role of the design consultant is not an easy one.

The specialized role of the corporate identity designer has evolved considerably since the early days of the profession. Today, he must create not only a logo but must also understand the company's operating, marketing, and financial strategies and must himself research strategic issues. The work is far more involved than making pretty pencil marks on a piece of paper.

The corporate identity designer must be able to translate the objectives of the company into a distinctive, memorable mark. Uniqueness is a quality that is very difficult to achieve in this day and age. In today's overcommunicated society, everything has been said once and seen at least twice. Aside from being distinctive and unique, the symbol must also maintain its clarity and integrity in one color, two colors, three colors, four colors; when embossed, foil-stamped; in step-repeat patterns (as seen on executive ties), in transit, on billboards, and so on. Applications (see chapter 8) will vary from company to company, depending on the nature and size of the firm.

Sometimes the executive reaction to a failing identity system is, "We need a new logo." Although a mark is an important part of a company's image, it alone does not constitute an identity program. Such a program is far more complex than a visual face-lift. The symbol created, in most cases, is not as important as its consistent application. A good symbol inconsistently applied is actually less effective than a weaker one that is consistently applied for all corporate-related materials. Any design consultant who sells a symbol alone as the complete corporate program is doing his profession and his client a disservice. The design consultant should let the client know the extent of the program immediately, as management does not always understand that much more than a new symbol is needed.

WHY CAN'T WE DO IT OURSELVES?

This is a question many company executives immediately ask themselves and the designer. Unless a company already has a sophisticated creative support staff, such as Apple Computers, or IBM, both companies that are known for their excellent design, it has neither the staff, facilities, nor expertise to create a design without the services of a corporate identity consultant. Just as a doctor diagnoses an illness, a design consultant must analyze a company's present condition to discover how it differs from the image the company wants to have—what is working and what is not.

FINDING THE RIGHT CONSULTANT

Once the need has been established, the initiator of the program (chief executive officer, advertising accounts executive, division manager, public relations officer, etc.) sets out to find a corporate identity designer. Finding the right consultant for the job can be an interesting and enlightening experience for any businessperson. It is important for designers to familiarize themselves with how and where he looks.

There are many trade magazines that feature the work of designers. *Print, Art Direction,* and *Communication Arts* are three leading American magazines. Each of these produces an annual featuring the work judged best in that year.

There are also national professional organizations, such as the American Institute of Graphic Arts or the Graphic Artists Guild, as well as regional and local organizations, such as the Art Directors Club of Los Angeles. These publish works of excellence in the field and supply lists of members. Directories such as the *American Art Directory,* the *Creative Black Book,* and the *L.A. Workbook* feature graphic designers in several fields, along with their areas of specialty.

Part of the designer's task is to familiarize management with the process of creating and implementing a successful program. The design consultant will bring years of specialized training, objectivity, and expertise to the project. He will guide management through the intricate decision-making process that will lead to a better understanding of the corporation's structure and goals, and he will provide a visual communications system that projects these objectives to various publics.

From the very beginning, good rapport should be established. Open lines of communication will create an atmosphere of ease and comfort that will lead to the overall effectiveness of the program. Designing for corporations is a very personal business. The selected consultant should be a person that management feels it can relate to, communicate with—a person whose judgment and experience can be trusted. As in any personal relationship, this commonality will be invaluable, when and if there are any conflicts.

As a consultant, the tendency toward objectivity is inherent in the fact that he is an outsider. He serves as a clinician who diagnoses, and it is entirely up to the patient whether or not to take the medication.

Advertising agencies will sometimes offer identity design work as an additional account capability. Hiring an advertising agency to do corporate identity design work is usually not a good idea for a variety of reasons. First, agencies usually do not have specialized staff experienced in the area and will usually "farm it out," passing on the increased cost to the client. Moreover, agencies lack the necessary detachment and objectivity, since they want to maintain the existing account and stay in the good graces of the company. A design consultant has no vested interest in simply telling management what it wants to hear.

Usually the client asks the possible consultant candidates for credentials, references, and samples of work on similar programs. It has not been proven important for a consultant to have had any direct previous experience in the particular business area. In fact, unfamiliarity with a business can be an advantage, providing the setting for fresh insight and original solutions.

A consultant should have the ability to understand a company's *basic nature* and to uncover meaningful relationships among seemingly dissimilar products, divisions, and subsidiaries. This requires the ability to understand an organization and communicate this understanding visually.

For the longest time designers have been engaged in an ongoing battle with marketing strategists. But a good designer is really a creative problem solver. He will keep in mind the true definition of the word design: "to conceive and plan out in the mind; to have as a purpose, to devise for a specific function or end; to conceive or execute a plan, to create, fashion, execute or construct according to the plan."[5] He will realize that a good design is not only a matter of attractiveness but also of functionality; and he will ask himself these questions: Is the design properly communicating the objectives of the firm to its target audiences? Is the message being systematically communi-

cated across every component of the system?

Designers must also be very good listeners. They must gain a complete understanding of what they are to communicate, and they must convey the company's history (past, present, and future) visually. To do this, they must be prepared to spend time not only with the initiator of the project but also with division managers as well as other employees; they are the ones who will be living with the operational aspects of the program.

Most designers are accustomed to the immediate gratification they get when a poster or publication is printed after it is designed; only a short period of waiting is involved. An identity design consultant must make a long-term commitment to the company if he is to see the program through successfully. The degree of involvement will depend greatly on the complexity of the problem and the size of the organization. The consultant hired should have the ability to supervise the implementation of the program. As the program gets underway, the level of the consultant's involvement should decrease. But the job requires tremendous attention to detail in order to ensure that the program does not lose momentum and that the intended objectives are communicated in unifying visual terms.

If the new identity is to be effective in the financial community and appealing to the investing public, the consultant should have a fundamental understanding of the company's economic environment. What is the price-earnings ratio of the stock? Has it risen in price?

Is there a growing number of shareholders? What are the major concerns of the security analysts? Have the firm's new products been successfully received? Is the company expanding into wider domestic or foreign markets?

Companies that are planning to operate outside the United States must be sure that their identities are appropriate for foreign markets. In international marketing each country should be studied for its attitudes toward visual devices, colors, and verbal themes. Before Standard Oil of New Jersey chose the name EXXON, ENCO was considered for use as its international symbol. ENCO was rejected when it was learned that the term actually means "stalled car" in Japanese.

Even for companies operating in this country, it is important to be certain that an identity will not have negative connotations for Americans with foreign backgrounds.

PROGRAM COSTS

The cost of a corporate identity program will vary from job to job, depending on several factors:

1. The size of the company. Larger and more complex organizations will usually require more work. As the complexity of the system increases, so does the consultant's fee.

2. The size of the consulting firm. Many corporate consultants are capable of guiding their clients through the entire program, including not only the evaluation of the market and the initial design but also interior design, packaging, collateral materials, and uniforms—a full range of capabilities.

3. The experience and reputation of the consultant. The more knowledgeable and well-established consultant can command higher fees for his services. This is a simple law of supply and demand. It is true that some firms will seek out the most expensive professional if the consultant has an established reputation.

4. Budget control. The consultant should operate in a businesslike fashion and be able to employ a systematic method of cost control. A budget should be submitted by the consultant prior to commencing any work. For a sample budget and proposal, see Appendix 1.

Proposals should be looked at very carefully by both parties, as the agreement will be contractually binding. Companies should determine whether the consultant has a reputation for completing programs within the original budget figure quoted, or if he frequently underbids in order to get the job. The firm should contact his previous clients to find out whether he kept to his earlier schedules and budget.

Fees can vary from $300 to $500 for a small individual identity program or for nonprofit organizations with limited identity applications and distribution, to $1.5 million or more for major corporations and Fortune 500 companies. Consultation fees can range from $30 to $250 per hour.

Some consultants will weigh the potential

growth of a firm against their initial fees; this is particularly true for new companies. An invaluable source for further information regarding pricing, as well as sample contractual agreements for the graphic designer, is the *Pricing and Ethical Guidelines,* published by the Graphic Artists Guild, 30 East 20th Street, New York, NY 10012.

STRUCTURE OF A DESIGN FIRM

Consulting firms—small and large—usually have a common structure. The complexity, budget, and extent of the identity program will dictate roles individuals will play in a particular project. The structure is flexible and varies from firm to firm. The flow of work usually travels as shown in the accompanying chart.

The accounts supervisor is usually an executive officer of the consulting firm and is experienced in account management. As David Ogilvy put it in his book, *Ogilvy on Advertising,* "He or (she) must be a good leader of frightened people. He must have financial acumen, administrative skill, thrust, and the courage to fire nonperformers. He must be a good salesman, because he is responsible for bringing in new clients. He must be resilient in adversity. Above all, he must have the physical stamina to work twelve hours a day, dine out several times a week, and spend half of his time in airplanes."

The accounts executive is responsible for maintaining contact with the client and nurtur-

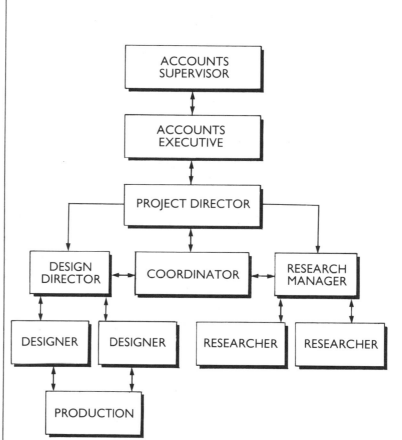

ing new business prospects. He usually "services" the account once the contract has been secured and is responsible for overseeing and delegating all work performed on the account by other departments.

A project director usually accompanies the accounts supervisor and the accounts executive on preliminary and subsequent client meetings. He must have an unusual set of characteristics: a background in graphic design (packaging, collateral, advertising, and so on), the ability to communicate effectively (using words and images), a strong analytical mind capable of strategic thinking, excellent administrative skills, and a good imagination.

The graphic designers must set very high standards for themselves and be not only creative but able to work under tremendous pressure, sustaining this rhythm for many hours. They must understand what possibilities exist in terms of typesetting, paper, and printing processes and should be able to communicate to the production artists specifications for translating their ideas into a printed piece. When working with graphic designers, project directors must keep in mind how difficult it is to be creative at all times, on all projects, and must manage their staffs accordingly. Many designers are overworked and should be given projects that vary in difficulty and the kind of commitment that is required.

4 TYPES OF SYMBOLS AND APPROACHES

There are many different types of symbols— linguistic, mathematical, scientific, and graphic. We encounter all of these on one level or another in our everyday lives. Certain symbols, such as the swastika (fig. 4-1), trigger immediate emotional responses. The swastika has been around since prehistoric times; it has changed names and crossed many cultural boundaries, meaning many things to different people. No one really knows where the swastika originated, but it has been found in ancient Crete on coins over three thousand years old, on Navajo artifacts, and on pre-Colombian pottery. In Sanskrit the word *swastika* means "all for one," connoting fertility and strength. The emblem suggests movement, representing the rays of the sun and the wind's four directions. These associations, which were once natural, organic, and benign, took on new meaning when the Nazis used the symbol as the centerpiece for their "corporate identity program" and turned its meaning into the modern-day equivalent of a skull and crossbones.

The power of a symbol lies in the effect it can have on the subconscious. A symbol may have positive or negative associations, and these associations operate on a deep subconscious level. Both Sigmund Freud and Carl Gustav Jung believed that symbols contain a logic and meaning that open the way to the understanding and resolution of problems or conflicts. This applies not only to personal problems but also to problems that can plague a corporation.

While there are symbols that can serve as effective tools in the marketplace, some symbols prove to do a company more harm than good (fig. 4-2). Procter & Gamble tried to squelch persistent rumors that their man-in the-moon symbol was satanic and that the company was somehow involved in devil worship. The company hired investigators to trace the origins of the rumor and even installed a toll-free number specifically for questions regarding the 103-year-old trademark.

The giant Cincinnati manufacturer finally decided to gradually remove the trademark from all of its products, which ranged from those for Crest toothpaste to those for Jif peanut butter. The symbol was obviously a hindrance and was no longer a company asset. This illustrates the psychological power of symbols. When an aritcle, product, service, or company is endowed with a symbol that has favorable associations, the company benefits from the positive associations.

Some symbols are immediately interpreted in particular ways. These are sometimes referred to as symbolic metaphors, or arche-

4-1. *The swastika, an ancient sign of fertility, became the visual keystone for Hitler's Third Reich. (Credit: American Marketing Association.)*

types. A bolt of lightning, for example, can symbolize speedy delivery, electrical currents, or messages from a higher authority. Stars can symbolize quality and distinction or can communicate pain.

A designer must be aware of the associations triggered by his forms. A drawing of a bird can at once communicate many different qualities. If it looks like a dove, it usually stands for peace, purity, or delicacy, as doves are associated with softness and femininity. If, on the other hand, the designer makes bolder strokes and the bird resembles a pigeon, it conjures up different associations—dirt, disarray, and the ordinary. Give the beak a downward tilt, and it resembles an eagle. Besides being the national bird of the United States, eagles connote the qualities of aggressiveness, righteousness, and courage (fig. 4-3).

During the Vietnam war in the sixties, when bank branches were being bombed, Bank of America instituted a campaign that depicted the bird in its symbol as a dove (fig. 4-4). The 1980s demand a different marketing game for banks, because of deregulation and competitive activity for the banking consumer. Bank of America has replaced the dove of the sixties with an eagle for the eighties, thereby conveying a completely different marketing stance simply through the use of imagery. "We put the eagle into the logo to symbolize leadership," says Charles Stewart, Bank of America's vice-president of marketing services. "It indicates that the bank is taking a more aggressive role in the marketplace."[6]

4-2. *Procter and Gamble tried unsuccessfully to squelch persistent rumors that their man-in-the-moon symbol was satanic and that the company was somehow involved in devil worship.*

4-3. *Bird figures drawn with slight differences can communicate different qualities.*

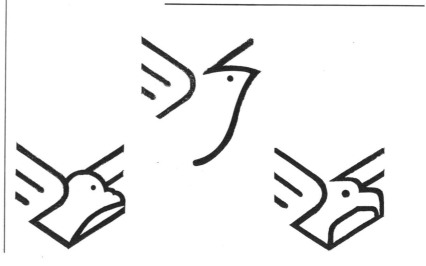

4-4. *The bird in the Bank of America symbol has been represented both as a dove and an eagle, each one conveying a completely different marketing stance through the use of promotional imagery.*

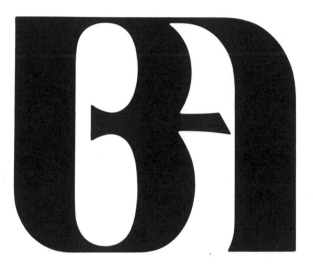

When people come into contact with a company, they usually have a subconscious response to that company's name or symbol. This response is then transferred to the company, its services, and/or its products. This phenomenon is known as *sensation transference*. A symbol, although it has an objective visual reality, always has a hidden and sometimes only partially intelligible meaning that has representational archetypical roots. Geometric symbols with sharp points are said to evoke a favorable effect on men; however, they have an undesirable effect on women. Symbols that are round or oval have a positive effect on both men and women. This could be attributed to the organic and nurturing qualities associated with roundness or curves.

BASIC SYMBOL CATEGORIES

Symbols can come in an infinite variety of shapes, forms, and colors. There is difficulty in distinguishing the difference between categories, as sometimes a symbol is comprised of several different approaches. Symbols can be typographic, abstract, descriptive, or a combination of these.

Typographic symbols use either the company name or its initials in a unique and distinct design (fig. 4-5). A *logotype* is created when only the company name is used in the design. A *seal*, on the other hand, is a word, group of words, or initials designed to fit inside a container or form. *Monograms* use the company's initials in a design devoid of a containing form.

The second category is an abstract approach. Abstract symbols usually represent images in a stylized, simplified manner. However, even in the most abstract symbols, representational images can sometimes be deciphered (fig. 4-6). The abstract symbol does not clearly refer to the organization it represents and will elicit associations only after the public has been exposed to it for some time. A large budget is therefore needed to promote recognition of an abstract mark.

During the sixties many corporations adopted abstract symbols, and the marketplace is now inundated with them. Uniqueness has become difficult to achieve because of the large number of existing designs that fall within this category. Abstract marks are usually associated with large organizations; an abstract mark for a company whose major objective is personalized service or attention would not be a very good choice.

A descriptive mark is one that relates a company's products or services representationally. This type of mark works successfully when it suggests the character of the organization, rather than shows actual products; products change over the years, and a symbol can become obsolete if it is too specific (fig. 4-7). Any one product reference can automatically exclude others, and combining several products rarely produces a satisfactory visual. Imagine, for instance, a chain of hardware stores that would try to depict a hammer, saw, and nail all in one symbol. A symbol is more

4-5. *Typographic symbols (from left to right):*
New York Life Insurance, by Lippincott and Margulies; Public
Broadcasting System, by Herb Lubalin; Exxon, by Raymond
Loewy; and Eaton, by Lippincott and Margulies.

4-6. Abstract symbols (from left to right):
Chase Manhattan Bank, by Chermayeff & Geismar Associates,
Herman Miller, by George Nelson & Company; North American
Rockwell, by Saul Bass & Associates; Pennwalt Corporation,
Gerald Stahl.

4-7. Descriptive symbols (from left to right):
AT&T, by Saul Bass and Associates; National Cotton Council, by
Landor and Associates; Jai-Alai, by Bud Jarrin; Eastern Airlines, by
Lippincott & Margulies.

valuable when it suggests the character of the organization rather than depicts the company's actual products.

WHICH SYMBOL IS BEST?

No specific formula can predict the success of a symbol, and designers and businessmen will often be at odds during the selection process. As solutions begin to emerge, the client and the design consultant must meet to integrate the creative process with the businessperson's firsthand knowledge of the company's prob-lems. As the best alternatives are identified, it is important to test their functional application by extending them onto various forms, such as letterhead, envelopes, and business cards (see chapter 7).

Designers tend to make bold, innovative choices, whereas businesspeople tend to choose conservative designs. The determining factor should be the ability of the symbol to communicate the company's objectives to its target market, which is the single most impor-tant function of a symbol.

5 METHODOLOGY—PHASE I

In planning a program, four basic steps can be taken both by the consultant and the client to achieve an effective design solution. Top management must be involved from the outset. If the identity program is to be effective, the chief executive officer must be aware that a problem exists and that it can be solved by a commitment to the program.

The basic steps of the process are:

Phase I: Analysis
Phase II: Design exploration
Phase III: Design refinement
Phase IV: Implementation

Designers will use only those steps that apply to the specific needs of the company. For example, a company may undertake a program and decide not to go ahead with the full implementation of it until several years after its completion.

The first phase of a program revolves around the definition of the identity problem or problems. This process consists of a series of evaluations through which the consultant and the client organize and gather all materials relevant to the company's problems, goals, and existing opportunities. Phase II sets the objectives of Phase I in motion by creating clear communication strategies. In other words,

Phase II is the point at which designers actually translate the communication objectives and strategies into a visual design. During Phase III the selected design concept is refined. The final phase, implementation, involves the systematic and consistent application of the system to all visual elements of the company, so that the public always encounters the company in the same visual terms.

PHASE I

The goal in this phase is to gather information, define problems, and establish objectives, paying particular attention to the internal structure of the company and how it is perceived by its key audiences (fig. 5-1). A shareholder, for instance, is likely to have a very different understanding of the company than an employee would. This analysis produces insights into problems and possible solutions. These appraisals can be conducted by using some or all of the following methods.

BRIEFING SESSIONS

Briefing sessions are a series of preliminary meetings at which the design consultant helps members of top-level management identify clear, concise communications objectives.

5-1. *The purpose of Phase I is to gather information, define problems, establish objectives, and analyze findings.*

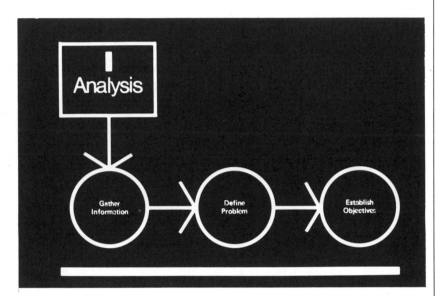

These will serve to guide his work through the remaining steps in the process. In its identity program, a company might want to demonstrate that it:

- provides products that are priced fairly.
- is progressive and innovative
- has excellent research-and-development facilities
- is known for natural products
- is profitable
- is expanding from regional to national to international
- has a diversified product line
- cares about public interest

INTERVIEWS

During the preliminary briefing sessions, the consultant and the client should agree on exactly whom the consultant should interview. Executive and employee interviews will help the consultant gain insight into:

- future directions for corporate growth
- marketing objectives and strategies
- the internal environment in which the identity will exist
- perceived corporate strengths and weaknesses
- employee attitudes toward corporate philosophy and policy
- present and future communication objectives

In addition, these interviews provide an invaluable insight into individual thinking and perceptions and have further important benefits.

For one, they allow management to participate and contribute at the beginning of the program. Managers rarely get the opportunity to review their sense of corporate philosophy and purpose, because they are involved in the daily grind of making the company run smoothly and are more concerned with profits. During this interview time, managers can focus their attention on communications as an integral part of long-term planning. A situation comes to mind in which the administrative officer was not involved in preliminary meetings and subsequent interviews. When it came time to design specific forms that were to be transmitted from office to office, the designer used the wrong dimensions and the forms could not be fed through one department's computer— a costly mistake that might have been averted if the operations manager had sat in on preliminary meetings. For this reason key managers (top, middle, and front-line) should be included among the interviewees. Their input and support is needed.

Many design consultants feel inadequate during this first phase, because they feel they lack a strong business sense. The more thorough their interviews, however, the less possibility of future errors and omissions. During these interviews, the consultant should not hold back, no matter how silly or inappropriate his questions may seem.

Typically, it is most effective to interview executives individually and in an informal setting. To maintain control over the direction of the interview, the design consultant should prepare a list of questions or a checklist and bring it to the sessions. But strict adherence to the outline is not necessary, as long as the pertinent questions are discussed.

Because these discussions may be somewhat revealing, the respondents must be assured that the information will be kept strictly confidential and that their responses will in no way endanger their positions with the company. This provides a nonthreatening atmosphere and invites the manager to talk freely about his perceptions. Most managers rarely get the chance to sit back and think about communication goals.

These interviews usually last anywhere from one to two hours each and cover the topics agreed on in the initial briefing. It is important to tape-record the interviews, so they can be reviewed, and specific information needed to support recommendations and findings can be extracted, at a later date.

QUESTIONNAIRES

An alternative to the interview process is a detailed questionnaire that is distributed to specific employees. This method is particularly useful when budget, geographical location, and time constraints do not permit personal interviews. The sample questionnaire found in Appendix 2 covers the basics. Each questionnaire should be tailored to specific projects and should incorporate any new leads that present themselves.

FACILITIES AUDIT

Exteriors, interiors, company equipment—virtually all structures that might use the company logo—are major vehicles for expressing a new identity. For example, the average truck-trailer combination yields almost 7.9 million visual impressions annually—about 101 visual impressions per driven mile. This establishes the power of a company fleet as a communications medium, since the visual impression is a communications and selling opportunity.

The design consultant must become familiar with the company's retail outlets, if any, finding out whom they serve, how space, colors, and ambient lighting within them is used, and how signage, both interior and exterior, is treated as an expression of the identity.

Photographing these outlets allows the consultant to study the situation and come up with missed identity opportunities. For example, by looking at photographs of Hayward Savings and Loan branches, the designer recognized the need for consistency in signage. Different typefaces were being used and the symbol was inconsistently applied (fig. 5-2).

GRAPHIC COMMUNICATIONS AUDIT

In order to complete the conceptual and creative problem-solving process, the design consultant must fully understand the visual environment in which a design must perform. Studying the company's printed communications will acquaint him with the printed image the company projects. At times, it can also provide insight about needless duplication and printing costs.

The project director employed by the design firm is usually responsible for collecting letterhead, photographs, house organs, marketing literature—virtually everything with the company's existing mark on it. The design consultant then mounts these on illustration boards by category (stationery, promotional items, marketing/sales literature, etc.), thus making the items easier to handle (fig. 5-3). (Sometimes he can end up with a studio full of everything from balloons to oil cans.) He will later take slides of the boards for client presentation. Mounting the items on boards also facilitates the viewing of the material by his team members and enables the client to study the material in a logical and sequential manner.

REVIEW EXISTING RESEARCH

In order to save time and money, the design consultant should request access to any research that was conducted by the company before initiating the identity program. Major companies within the same industry often encounter similar difficulties; some related research data is therefore usually available for a specific problem. This information can be obtained by reading trade journal articles, contacting industry organizations, and reviewing existing research statistics.

ADDITIONAL RESEARCH

If all the steps taken fail to provide adequate insight into the attitudes, needs, and percep-

5-2. *By looking at photographs of Hayward Savings and Loan branch offices, the designer recognized the need for consistency in signage. Different typefaces had been used and the symbol had been inconsistently applied. (Credit: Communications Planning.)*

5-3. *The design consultant mounts all of the items collected with a company's existing mark on illustration boards by category, thus making the items easier to handle.*

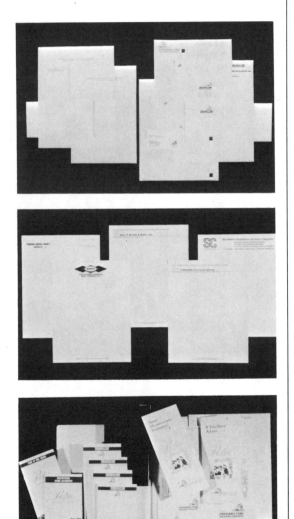

tions of a company's key audiences and objectives, additional research can be conducted: the client can contract with an independent research firm, the design consultant can hire his own team of researchers, or he can assist the client in the hiring process. Many large consulting firms have their own in-house facilities that may include test kitchens, simulated grocery store shelves, and qualitative/quantitative research facilities.

Design research (both image and packaging) is an analytical tool that uses a variety of techniques. There are two main techniques—ocular and verbal tests.

Ocular tests determine what individuals see, the length of time they focus on the object, which elements attract the eye, and which elements are ignored. These tests measure physiological rather than emotional responses to visual stimuli.

A *tachistoscope* is used to test and measure visibility, legibility, recognition, and recall by throwing an image on a screen for a brief measured period (usually a fraction of a second). The eye-tracker uses an infrared light, which bounces off the participant's eye and is superimposed directly onto the material being viewed. Initially, images are flashed on a screen at approximately 1/100 of a second; the exposure is gradually increased, until the images on the screen can be identified.

The tachistoscope pinpoints whether consumers are drawn to the design, or, more important, whether they are completely ignoring it.

Designers find the tachistoscope a useful device in predesign and postdesign activities, since it allows them to understand if the key elements of the design are being seen by the consumer.

Verbal tests, on the other hand, are easier to administer than those that use a machine. Because of their flexibility, verbal tests can be conducted in shopping centers, hotel rooms, advertising agencies, by telephone, or in sidewalk interviews. Questions in a verbal test might go as follows:

1. Look at this symbol and tell me what it means to you?
2. Does it remind you of anything?
3. What does it communicate about the company it represents?
4. Would you buy any products that this company manufactures?
5. Is there anything about the symbol that you do not like?
6. How do you feel about the colors?
7. How do you feel about the legibility of the logotype?
8. How does this symbol compare with symbols in similar industries?

The same questions should be asked about each of the favored design directions. After questioning the participant about all of the favored directions, final questions can then be asked, such as:

1. Which design has the strongest appeal?

2. What is the one thing about your favored design that appeals to you the most?
3. Which design has the second highest appeal? What is its strongest point?

The interviewer should probe to elicit the most extensive reply and should record the participant's answers. The designer should look for patterns in the response to the questions and should summarize the findings in order to draw conclusions and make recommendations to his client.

A *focus group* discussion consists of a group of anywhere from six to ten carefully selected consumers who have demonstrated interest in the product or service being tested. These individuals usually base their responses on first-hand experience. Obviously, the easier it is to gather a selected group, the less expensive the process. Family households driving American cars, for example, would be easier to sample than architects who have had kidney operations.

The participants are selected on the basis of demographics: age, sex, marital status, and income. Some research groups have even included life-style profiles in their screenings by asking questions about consumer habits, educational background, occupation, travel experience, and hobbies.

The respondents meet in a relaxed, unstructured environment. The group leader, or moderator, usually gives a brief introduction and then discusses specific problems related to the project, based on a prepared outline. The responses are usually videotaped for review at a later date. The sessions can last anywhere from one-and-one-half to two hours. Depending on the facilities, a two-way mirror allows clients, designers, and other members of the research group to follow the discussions without being seen. The opportunity to directly participate and ask questions is facilitated by the two-way mirror. Questions that had not been thought of previously can be addressed by simply sending a note to the moderator.

Focus group discussions can reveal many consumer attitudes, generate new ideas, add to the information collected, and reveal potential strengths and weaknesses of the organization or product being tested. The basic difference between the individual interview and the focus group is that the individual interview is stimulated only by the interviewer. In a group interview, each individual is exposed not only to the moderator but to the ideas of the group as well. At the end of the session, the moderator summarizes the findings and asks the participants for conclusions.

ANALYSIS OF FINDINGS— PRESENTATION TO CLIENT

All the information gathered from executive interviews, a facilities audit, a graphic communications audit, existing research reviews, and any additional research must be integrated and analyzed. This is the final step before a design consultant can develop clear identity objectives and opportunities.

Findings are presented to management, usually in slide format, accompanied with a written document that duplicates the slide presentation. At this presentation the designer should be prepared to recommend specific communication and design objectives for strengthening the existing identity or creating a new one.

By the end of the meeting, an agreement should be reached about specific communication and design objectives. These will become the criteria that guide the creative exploration and the subsequent evaluation of the design directions the consultant will suggest.

6 DESIGN EXPLORATION—PHASE II

Design exploration is the creative portion and the heart of any corporate identity program. Graphically, most identity projects fall into one of three categories:

- the modification of an existing identity
- the creation of an identity for a newly formed company
- the creation of a new identity for an established company

DEVELOPING A CONCISE DESIGN BRIEF

A clear definition of all marketing criteria will help the design team meet the communication objectives successfully and with minimal expenditure. Changes that result from the project director's inability to communicate design objectives to the designers on the job can add 20 to 60 percent or more in design costs to the original budget.

Once the communication objectives have been established, the project director is in a position to outline all the specifics in writing, so designers can begin work on the project. The project director prepares a written report, or design brief, explaining the scope of the project and its market communications objectives. The brief should also include information about the company's background, its organizational structure, the competition, its marketing and advertising plans, the project's technical requirements, any research findings, and proposed images.

COMPANY BACKGROUND

As much detail as possible should be provided about the background of a company—how, where, when, and why the company was formed. Is it a family-owned, privately owned, or a public operation? Attention should be paid to existing problems—what were the reasons for initiating an identity program? It is also useful to provide the design team with old annual reports, newspaper clippings about the company, and other material that might contain some background information on the company.

ORGANIZATIONAL STRUCTURE OF THE COMPANY

Graphs that depict the organization of the company—its products, divisions, subdivisions—can be a useful tool for the designer. This will enable him to see and understand the internal hierarchy, as well as the role and rela-

6-1. *The information provided in the design brief might include samples of the competition's existing identities.*

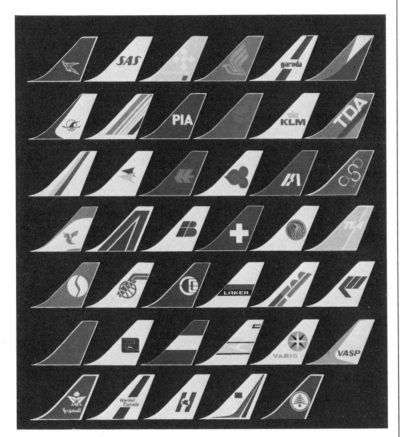

tionship of the products and divisions to the parent organization.

COMPETITIVE ACTIVITY

In order for the design team to be fully aware of the strengths and weaknesses of the competition and to be able to spot strategic opportunities for the company, they should receive information about the competition. This information might include samples of the competition's existing identity, material about the competition's marketing and advertising activities, and trade articles (fig. 6-1). As the old proverb goes, "Know thine enemy."

MARKETING AND ADVERTISING PLANS

Past, present, and future marketing plans should also be included in the brief. The designer should understand where the company has been and where it is going, so that he can develop meaningful design solutions that will anticipate market trends. Copies of current print ads, promotional material, or any recent advertising material will also help the designer understand the company's future plans for promotion (fig. 6-2).

TECHNICAL REQUIREMENTS

Before the designer begins to develop design concepts, he must understand the technical parameters of the project. Specific uses for the symbol should be mapped out, as these will have an effect on the final concept.

RESEARCH FINDINGS

A distillation of the research conducted to date should be provided for the designer's use. This will help him understand the consumer's perceptions about the product, service, or company.

POSSIBLE IMAGE DIRECTIONS

Designers rarely accompany the team on preliminary meetings and must therefore gain an understanding of the project through the eyes of the project or design director. It is best to begin with an image that will be familiar to the targeted audience. For example, a small local bank is located in an area that is identified regionally by a historical landmark—a lighthouse. If one of the marketing objectives of that bank were to grow from a small local bank to a statewide bank, then the lighthouse—an image that would be recognized around the state—would be appropriate. Communicating details about appropriate imagery to the designer makes his job easier to do. After all, there are many ways to draw a lighthouse—stylized, pictorial, abstract—but all might not be in keeping with the bank's communication objectives (fig. 6-3).

Regardless of whether a design consulting firm has two hundred employees or two, a brief provides the designer with a written statement of purpose. The more information designers have, the easier it will be for them to accomplish meaningful and economical design solutions. A sample of a design brief can be found in Appendix 3.

6-2. Examples of existing promotional material can be helpful in terms of providing an insight into the company's future plans and opportunities for promotion.

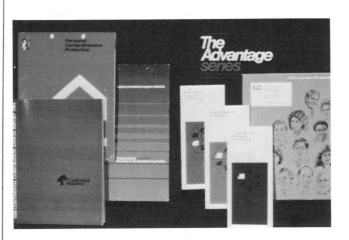

6-3. There are many ways to draw a lighthouse—pictorially or abstract—that might or might not be in keeping with the communication objectives.

6-4. *Symbols evolve over a period of time, reflecting a company's direction and growth.*

1896

1900s

1920s

1940s

1950s

1970s

1977

1984

PRACTICAL CONSIDERATIONS WHEN DESIGNING A SYMBOL

In addition to keeping specific design objectives in mind, designers must also consider durability when creating a symbol. Typefaces and images that are trendy should be avoided, as they can quickly become obsolete. On the other hand, a symbol that is memorable, distinct, and unique within the industry for which it was created will be able to stand the test of time (fig. 6-4).

A company's present and possible future activities must be kept in mind; one that is going through a period of mergers and acquisitions requires a design flexible enough to accommodate these changes.

The design should be reproducible on all types of surfaces, papers, and in every situation imaginable. It is therefore best to keep the design simple—symbols that reproduce well in black and white with a minimum number of lines. If the design has too many tones, chances are it will lose its clarity in certain applications, such as in newspapers, magazine advertisements, and so on (fig. 6-5).

The design must also work in a variety of sizes; it should be legible when reduced down to an eighth of an inch, yet effective on a billboard as well. To achieve this, the designer must treat the black (positive) and white (negative) spaces as additional elements in the design. For example, if there is too little white space, the area will fill in when the image is reduced, rendering the symbol illegible. Line weights should be looked at closely and adjusted for reduction and enlargement.

KEYS TO CREATIVITY

As children we were taught that there is only one right answer. This attitude is deeply ingrained in our thinking and our approach to problem solving. One of the first things that a designer must do if involved during this phase of creativity is understand that there are many solutions to a problem. Many people regard innovation and creative thinking as entirely too much work, when it should be looked upon as fun and challenging.

Certain methods can be used by the designer during this exploratory phase to stretch the imagination and ease the conceptual design phase. There is no "sure fire" best technique —only that which works best for the individual.

PRELIMINARY SKETCHING METHOD

The designer should start by doing some small sketches called *thumbnails* (½ to 1 inch in size). This allows the designer to work quickly and produce a large quantity of ideas in a short period of time. Ideas can be quickly evaluated without getting into too much detail. A tracing pad and either a #2 or 2B pencil can be used to sketch out the ideas. The ideas that are the most promising are strengthened with a black felt-tipped marker or technical pen (fig. 6-6).

One of the best time- and money-saving techniques used by designers is the paper copier. During this preliminary stage, it is easier to

6-5. *If the design has too many tones, chances are it will lose its clarity in certain applications (such as a telephone book advertisement).*

6-6. *The designer should start by doing some small sketches with few details. This allows him to work quickly and experiment with many ideas. (Credit: Communications Planning.)*

6-7. These symbols were all created with the help of a photocopier. By respacing and slightly modifying the bar and petals, variations of the symbol were created.

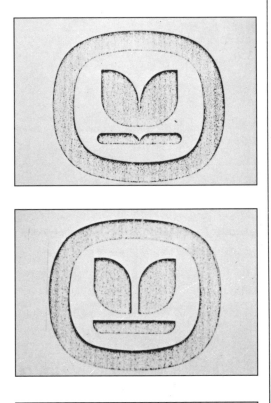

use copies than photostatted images. Photostats are considerably more expensive and are used extensively during the refinement of a symbol (Phase III). Copiers are quick and allow the designer more time to conceptualize; he saves time not having to redraw ideas. Some copiers allow for variable sizes and can print on larger paper (11 by 17 inches). Images can be enlarged, reduced, and condensed (with a special lens attachment). Images can then be respaced, cut apart, pieced together, and copied again (fig. 6-7). Type specimen books can be used to trace type, placed on the copier and be enlarged or reduced, and used to create logotypes; or they can be used to study the symbol-to-logotype relationship. White artist's tape or typewriter correction fluid can be used to cover up unwanted areas of black. Black areas can be strengthened by going over them with a felt-tipped marker and then having them recopied.

Designers should find a conveniently located copier with enlarging and reducing capabilities. If a copier is not available, tracing can also be a useful tool for copying images. Using a light table or any other form of readily available light (window), designs can be traced; the designer can quickly improve the sketch by either exluding or including any new ideas.

ATTRIBUTE ANALOGY CHAINS
Ideas are often found by incorporating two or more concepts. By writing down all of a company's attributes, the designer can begin to

force relationships between the alternative images.

Example: The project is to redesign the brand identity for a new sourdough bread baked in San Francisco.

First, the designer lists as headings the qualities that are to be conveyed by the new design. Below each of these attributes, he lists alternative images for visually reinforcing that quality. He then makes systematic combinations by taking one attribute from each list and assembling the combinations into a design.

6-8. *In this design for San Francisco French Bread, designer Nash Hernandez uses seagulls and a nautical theme reminiscent of Fisherman's Wharf. He uses an old Western typeface for the words San Francisco, recalling the city's rich heritage. The words are surrounded by bands of color resembling ribbons, and the name Earth Grains is superimposed on a bale of wheat.*

Objectives/Attributes

<table>
<tr><td rowspan="6" style="writing-mode: vertical-rl">Alternative Image Sources</td></tr>
<tr><td>HISTORICAL ROOTS</td><td>SYMBOLS OF QUALITY</td><td>NATURAL IMAGES</td></tr>
<tr><td>Golden Gate</td><td>Crowns</td><td>Baker</td></tr>
<tr><td>Barbary Coast</td><td>**Ribbon**</td><td>Farm</td></tr>
<tr><td>**Fisherman's Wharf**</td><td>Crests</td><td>**Staff of Wheat**</td></tr>
<tr><td>Gold Rush</td><td>Stars</td><td>Chef's Hat</td></tr>
</table>

To take the process a step further, the designer can render each design in each of the different design categories: typographic, abstract, and descriptive (fig. 6-8).

MANIPULATING WORDS

The relationships among words, their sounds and meanings, can also be a valuable source for designers to explore. Many contemporary designers use letterforms to create designs. A designer should be well versed in typography

and should consider the content and meaning of words, in addition to the way they are arranged. For over forty years, Herb Lubalin designed elegant and sophisticated typography-based design. For example, there is a child in his logo for *Mother & Child* and a family in *Families* (fig. 6-9).

VISUAL RESEARCH

The search for visual concepts can sometimes be laden with frustration. Once the research and analysis portion of the program is completed, the designer must seek images that will lead to the final concept.

Illuminating ideas can sometimes surface when the designer is completely detached from the problem, both physically and mentally. Art museums, galleries, and nature can provide the required visual nourishment that can encourage and stimulate the imagination. Looking at related design objects, such as furniture, modern art, or a sculpted landscape, can sometimes get the creative juices flowing.

Symmetry and design are everywhere in nature—flowers, shells, birds. Many creative solutions to design problems are adapted from natural forms. Logarithmic spirals used in columns can be traced back to their form in nature—a shell (fig. 6-10).

Design solutions to similar problems might also be inspired by reviewing old publications and design manuals. The most obvious disadvantage to this method is that they may encourage imitation instead of imagination. Because of this, journals are sometimes referred to in the trade as "swipe files." On the other hand, they can provide the designer with insight and can encourage a new approach to the design problem.

Another option is to create an "image bank" that contains clipped-out images found in magazines, books, or photographs that are particularly appealing to the designer. Over the years he can accumulate quite a library of material. In addition, sketches that were used for previous projects should be saved for future reference. The image bank should include doodles as well as tight sketches from previous jobs. These sketches should be kept, as they remain the exclusive property of the designer. By going back into these files, a designer might be able to take a big leap forward, finding the seed of an idea that can provide the answer to a current problem.

COLOR AND CORPORATE COMMUNICATION

The graphic symbol, the logotype, and the use of color are the visual elements that constitute a corporate identity program. Color can serve as a tool that links divisions and brands to the parent company. Color adds a new dimension to corporate communication. It gives the symbol life, accentuates certain qualities, and facilitates perception, awareness, and recall.

As in the creative exploration of symbols, many variations of color and color combinations should be tested to determine which ones best describe the activities and objectives of the organization.

6-10. *Many design solutions are derived from natural forms. Logarithmic spirals used in columns can be traced back to the shell.*

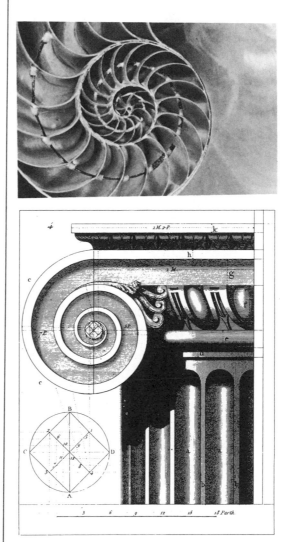

6-11. *The Kodak package makes effective use of two colors. It is a most successful packaging scheme that has helped the company corner the photographic market for many decades.*

Many studies on color in the marketplace have been published, but no definitive source explains the meaning of color in every use and in every context, as these vary considerably from culture to culture. The list in Appendix 4 has been compiled to aid the graphic designer when selecting color and color combinations for different products, services, or organizations. Different combinations of color can evoke emotional responses. For example, when combined with red, yellow, which is said to subliminally suggest a need for something new and modern, might suggest a desire to conquer new horizons. The Kodak package makes effective use of these two colors (fig. 6-11); no doubt it is a most successful packaging scheme that has contributed to the company's cornering of the photographic market for many decades.

The objective of color is always the same: it imparts information, sells the product, and creates lasting identity. When associated with a corporation or its products, color can improve identification and add suggestive imagery and symbolic value.

COMPUTER-GENERATED DESIGN

The computer is now a tool available to the designer. The first computers processed only text; newer devices support graphics, color (more than 1,000 colors and shades on the screen at any time, from a palette of 64,000 colors), and even three-dimensional shape manipulation and shading. Development of these features began in the 1960s; they were first commonly used in the late 1970s, with the large-scale introduction of microprocessor-based computers and graphic workstations. These devices, which range in price from $4,000 to $100,000, have changed the way the graphic designer explores design concepts and prepares material for client presentation. A very sophisticated computer graphics system can produce slides, prints, and color separations.

Relatively inexpensive user-friendly systems can perform complex graphic functions with a keyboard and a graphic input device, such as a light pen, digitizing tablet, mouse, or graphic scanner. These devices make freehand drawing on the computer possible. The *light pen* looks like a pen and serves the same function when it is held against the screen of the computer. Whenever you "draw," the computer follows with a line. A light pen can also be used to erase, shade, and fill in shapes.

The *digitizing tablet* also consists of a penlike object. It is applied to a plastic tablet, which in turn translates the positional information into lines and shapes on the computer screen. This is the most effective manual device for reproducing shapes with a computer.

The *mouse* is a small boxlike device that is moved around a desk top by hand. In addition to its uses as a drawing tool, the mouse contains keys that are used to give commands to the computer.

Another device available for input to a graphic computer is the *graphic scanner*. Scanners use either a television camera or a line-scan device (which resembles a computer) for transferring drawings to the computer screen without tracing. The television camera allows three-dimensional objects to be represented on the computer screen.

We will use the following logo as an example of computer-aided design. A photocopy of the sketch was scanned into the computer and, using a scan command, was reduced by about 20 percent (fig. 6-12).

The logo then becomes part of a computer file, where it can be altered in a variety of ways (fig. 6-13). It can be framed in square shapes of differing thicknesses and then electronically cut and pasted in different patterns. The file can then be printed, and the preferred symbol variation refined manually and later implemented (fig. 6-14).

A basic element such as the ballerina shown is first drawn on a piece of tracing paper (fig. 6-15), then photocopied and scanned into the computer screen (fig. 6-16). Different shading screens can be used; the figure can be duplicated and positioned at various angles (fig. 6-17) and placed in perspective, distorting the limbs (fig. 6-18). The desired design can then be selected and printed (fig. 6-19).

Computers allow designers to manipulate an image without altering it permanently. Perhaps most important, computers make it easier for the designer to prepare many different options for clients to consider without laboring forever on an idea that will be dropped at a later stage.

The computer also permits the building and

6-12. *Symbols can be manipulated on a computer, saving the designer hours of creative time.*

6-13. *The logo then becomes part of a computer file, where it is altered in a variety of ways. (Credit: Communications Planning.)*

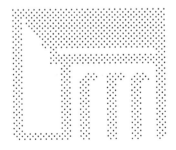  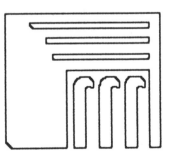

6-14. *The logo can then be printed, refined manually, and later implemented as shown here. (Credit: Communications Planning.)*

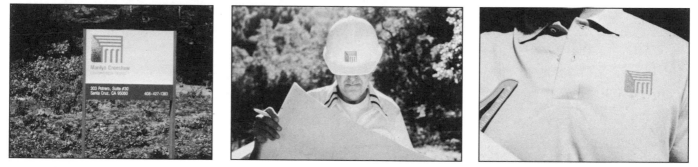

6-15. *A basic element such as this ballerina is first drawn on a piece of paper and photocopied.*

6-16. *Then the figure is scanned into the computer.*

6-17. *Different shading screens can be used, and the figure can be duplicated and positioned at various angles.*

6-18. *The figure can be placed in perspective by distorting the limbs.*

6-19. *The desired design is then selected, printed out, and reproduced. (Credit: Communications Planning.)*

Volume I, Number 2   Spring 1986

CONTENTS

Marin Review
Hal Landon, Editor
Veronica Napoles, Art Director

Marin Arts Council
Yandex Johnson, Executive Director
Roni Simon, Program Manager

1986 Board of Directors
Joanne Dunn, President
Pat Terell-Smith, Vice-President
Phyllis Thelen, Secretary
Alice May, Treasurer
Harold C. Brown, Jr.
Dan Caldwell
Jody Crosier
Chuck Conley
Maryjane Dunstan
Mark Fishkin
Warren Franklin
Maxwell McCoy-Buck
Beulah Kerry
Bruce Lauritzen
Joan Peterson
Ann Stephens
Diane E. Navarre Doolin
Don Taves
Ken Todd
Travis Underwood
Ivy Wellington

Printing by Marin Sun
Typesetting by Hillside Setting

Marin Review is a quarterly publication of the Marin Arts Council which is mailed free to members. © copyright 1986 Marin Arts Council. All rights reserved.

The Marin Review is supported by membership contributions and grants from the San Francisco Foundation, the California Arts Council, and the National Endowment for the Arts. The Marin Arts Council offices are located at 251 North San Pedro Rd., San Rafael, CA 94903. (415) 499-8350.

On the Cover: Jay Daniel is a photographer doing corporate and editorial work from his studio in industrial San Rafael. Besides working with a number of national accounts, he is also known for his series of black and white nudes, "Naked Cafe." Daniel photographed author Molly Giles with a Canon F1 (35mm) using an 85-mm F1.8 lens and Kodak Pan-X film.

Illustration of computerized ballerina: Michael Kiverman

MARIN REVIEW SPRING 1986 3

retention of a graphic library of elements and images, which can be easily combined with each other and with original art.

Less than ten years ago, the newspaper editorial room was a clatter of typewriters (often manual), with dozens of steps between the initial typewritten word and ultimate newsprint and ink. Today, in fully automated editorial offices, original copy is typed, edited, and laid out on a computer screen; a computer-directed laser beam can even expose plates.

Today most graphic artists and designers work with pencil and ink on paper and tissue. Perhaps in ten years, when lower costs make computers more accessible, most graphic designers will work with computers, freeing them to explore new graphic concepts.

PRESENTATION TO CLIENT

Phase II concludes with a presentation of sketches to the client. At this meeting, all work (including small thumbnails) should be shown to the client. Several typefaces should be used in combination with the marks in photocopy form. This way the client can begin to visualize the symbol in combination with a typeface. Sketches should be organized in a way that allows for easy viewing. The symbols can be mounted on boards (using a consistent paper size with lots of room around each sketch) or photographed and presented in slide format. The designer should be prepared to discuss the relative merits of each of the sketches and make recommendations, singling out the most promising designs.

7 DESIGN REFINEMENT—PHASE III

During the refinement stage, the basic design direction is approved. The designer takes a closer look at the preferred design concepts presented in Phase II. Approved rough sketches showing the basic elements of the mark are then taken a step further and improved.

In this example (fig. 7-1), the client and the designer agreed during Phase II that the images of the flask and the stalks of wheat seemed to be the most promising direction for Nutri-search, a pharmaceutical company that manufactures natural health-care products. Both felt that the flask combined with the stalks of wheat would produce a symbol that was too long; it would take up too much space when printed on the company's existing product labels. In the next step, Phase III, the designer redrew the symbol, this time inverting the stalks into the flask, thereby reducing the length of the mark, and began to explore variations of the mark (fig. 7-2). The symbol was combined with the company name and drawn slightly off-center (fig. 7-3). The symbol was placed to the left of the company name (fig. 7-4). A container was added around the flask, creating a monoseal (fig. 7-5). A negative version of the preceding symbol was created and centered over the company name (fig. 7-6).

The mark or marks that the designer intends to recommend to the client should be drawn accurately with technical pens as large as 6 by 6 inches. A slightly reduced photostat should then be made of the tightly drawn mark. Photostatting is a method of photographically reproducing flat black-and-white art to any size. It is an extremely clean method of reproduction, available in both paper and film. A photostat camera can also reproduce images in either a positive or negative (reverse) form. The photostatted mark should be singly mounted on an illustration board for presentation (fig. 7-7).

The symbol can be overlooked by the client or not fully appreciated if it is presented without first showing the symbol in different applications. A good mark should be able to work in many different applications. Therefore, comprehensive or prototypical mock-ups of the mark should now be constructed to represent the design as it would appear in printed pieces (letterhead, envelopes, business cards), vehicles, packages, and so on. Creating prototypes enables the clients to visualize how the design will work and look in real-life situations. Depending on the proposal submitted by the designer, either one, two, three, or four final concepts are refined and presented to the client as prototypes.

Designers can create mock-ups in many ways to communicate his visual solutions to the client. It does take time and money to prepare

7-1. *The image of the flask and stalks of wheat seemed to be the most promising design solution for Nutrisearch.*

7-2. *In the next step the designer redrew the symbol, inverting the stalks into the flask, thereby reducing the length of the mark.*

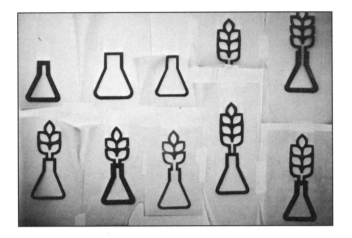

7-3. *The symbol was combined with the company name and drawn slightly off-center.*

7-4. *The symbol was placed to the left of the company name.*

7-5. *A container was added around the flask, creating a monoseal.*

7-6. *A negative version of the preceding symbol was created and centered over the company name. (Credit: Communications Planning.)*

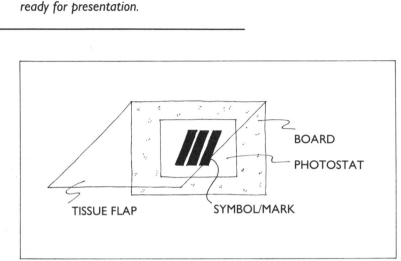

comprehensives, and techniques will vary. A designer can present ideas informally by simply using colored pencils to re-create the mark onto letterhead, envelopes, and business cards; to present them elaborately, he can mock-up the proposed mark with custom rubdown transfers of the symbol on everything from letterhead to employee pins. The techniques used on each identity job will depend on the budget, the company's needs, and the designer's own particular style of presentation.

MOCK-UP TECHNIQUES

Colored pencils can produce a fairly accurate comprehensive on smooth paper. The designer can keep the pencil sharpened and produce tight, detailed drawings. Different colors can be created by blending pencil colors. Excess color can be easily scraped off by using an X-acto knife lightly.

Felt-tipped markers can cover large areas quickly, but the color can be uneven and will easily smear if used on tracing paper. Markers do have the advantage of enabling the designer to do quick color studies of the symbols before committing to one color combination.

Colored films profide a smooth transparent layer of color. The artwork to be colored is placed on a light table with a piece of the colored film on top. Colored films have an adhesive back and will stick to the artwork. Care must be taken in placing the film, as removal of the film could destroy the underlying artwork. The designer then outlines the area to be colored with an X-acto knife, and the excess film is removed. A burnisher is used to secure the colored film to the artwork. Available in sheets at most art-supply stores, the films are matched to printing inks and come in a variety of colors.

The technique of custom rubdown transfers uses the same principle as rubdown transfer type. Photostats of the symbol(s) at different sizes and with different type are pasted up on a board. Depending on the size of the board (5 by 7 inches, 8 by 10 inches, 11 by 17 inches), designers tightly squeeze as many of the images as they want in rubdown form. Custom transfers are also matched to printing inks and come in a wide range of colors. This technique is expensive, and designers are charged per sheet, size, and number of colors ordered. Color transfers can then be burnished down onto paper stock, creating mock-up pieces that closely approximate the actual printed piece. (The letterhead in figure 7-8 was prepared with custom rubdown transfers of the symbol and typeface in three different colors.)

Blind embossing can be simulated by cutting the symbol out of the same paper it is to be glued onto (fig. 7-9). A symbol can also be mocked up to look as though it had been foil-stamped (fig. 7-10). To achieve this the symbol is cut out of foil paper and glued to background paper, which can be in any color.

SYSTEMS DESIGN

Letterhead, envelopes, and business cards are usually the first elements completed in the process of creating a new identity. A systematic use of the identity can be easily conveyed to the client with these items.

7-8. This letterhead was mocked up using custom rubdown transfers of the symbol and typeface in three different colors. (Credit: Communications Planning.)

7-9. *Blind embossing can be simulated by cutting the symbol out of the same paper to which it is to be glued.*

7-10. *A symbol can also be mocked up to look as though it had been foil-stamped.*

The standard size for letterhead in the United States is 8½ by 11 inches. The "monarch" paper size is slightly smaller (7¼ by 10½ inches) and is used occasionally by company executives for personalized notes and memos. Envelopes come in a variety of sizes, but the one most commonly used in everyday business activities is the #10 envelope (4⅛ by 9½ inches). Business cards also come in a variety of sizes, but the most common size used is 2 by 3½ inches. Some designers prefer to use larger or smaller sizes when creating cards for their clients. The major disadvantage to this technique is that the cards usually will not fit in the standard filing system for business cards. The oddly sized card designed to stand out could get lost or, worse yet, discarded.

To design a system for a company, the designer starts with basic design elements (symbol, type, color) and creates as many layout variations as possible. By working small, many variations can be explored quickly. Each of the following are approximately 2 inches long (fig. 7-11).

When all layout possibilities are exhausted, the designer should choose the one that shows the most promise and evaluate it by looking at:

• Flexibility: Does the design lend itself to being easily extended onto other applications?
• Information: Is all the required copy (company name, address, city, state, zip code, telephone number, name, and title) included on the items?

• Consistency: Are all design elements consistent on all the pieces?

The identity should unify an entire range of an organization's corporate-related materials (packages, signage, annual reports, advertising, and so on). Each application of the mark is a design problem on its own. However, a solid design system will provide a strong foundation and starting point for each of these applications.

In creating an identity system for Fireman's Fund Corporation, the design firm Communications Planning explored different stationery layouts (fig. 7-12). The chosen layout was then used as a model and applied consistently to all stationery, forms, and brochures throughout the company (fig. 7-13).

PRESENTATION TO CLIENT

At this presentation the designer will present the symbol(s) in final form. His purpose should be to convince the client to approve one of the symbol directions. The designer should explain how he arrived at that symbol. The discussion should be kept relative to the client's marketing objectives established in Phase I. Presentation at this stage of the identity program can be informal (fig. 7-14); showing the finished symbol along with the preferred stationery layout is sufficient. Or the designer may choose a more elaborate presentation and show the symbol mocked up in a variety of applications (fig. 7-15).

7-11. *By working small, many variations of a design can be explored quickly.*

7-12. In creating an identity system for the Fireman's Fund Corporation, different stationery layouts were explored. (Credit: Communications Planning.)

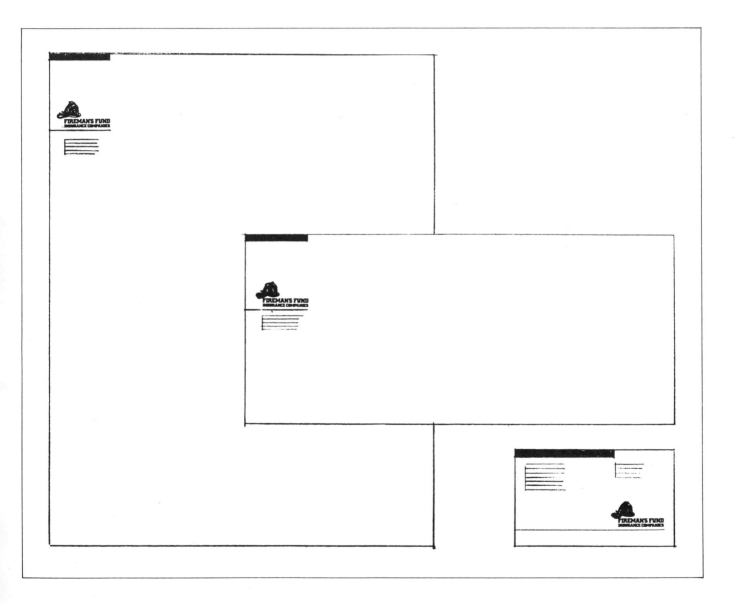

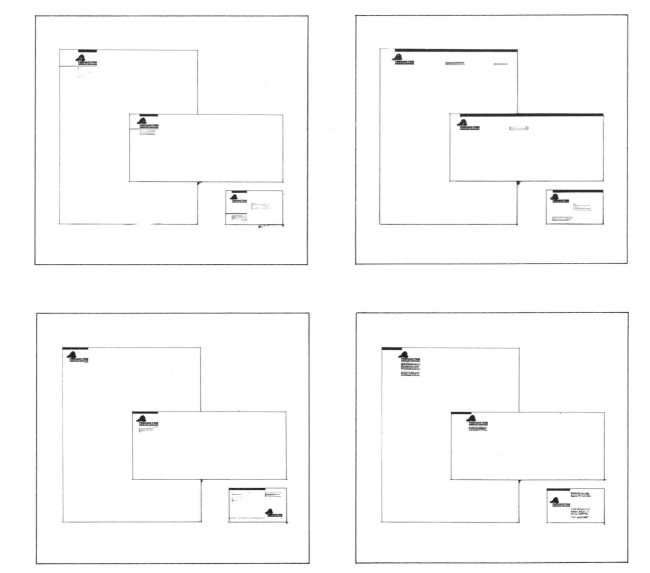

7-13. The chosen layout was then used as a model and applied consistently to all stationery, forms, and brochures throughout the company. (Credit: Communications Planning.)

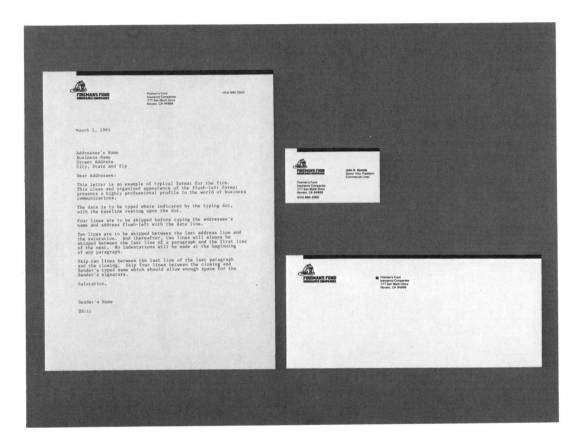

7-13 *(cont.)*

7-14. *Presentation at this stage of the identity program can be informal, showing the finished symbol along with the preferred stationery layout. (Credit: Communications Planning.)*

7-15. The designer may choose a more elaborate presentation and show the symbol mocked up in a variety of applications.

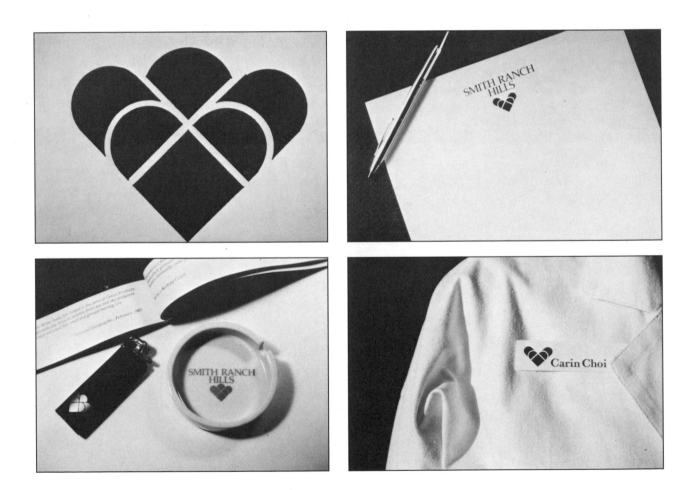

Some designers feel that the more applications used to illustrate the symbol during this phase, the more chance there is of client acceptance for the design solution. The designer should keep in mind that an effective presentation is one that communicates to the client what he needs to know about the designer's ideas.

8 IMPLEMENTATION—PHASE IV

THE CORPORATE IDENTITY MANUAL

The first corporate identity manual was produced approximately thirty years ago. Since then, thousands of small and large corporations have discovered the need for a graphic standards manual.

A manual becomes the bible for the consistent application of the identity throughout all corporate materials. Without one, an identity program becomes difficult, if not impossible, to manage, especially if the printing, buying, ordering, and specification of corporate-related materials is not a centralized function.

The standards manual covers everything from stationery, signage, and advertising, all the way down to employee five-year pins. This assures that every time someone comes into contact with the organization, its identity is communicated in the same visual terms.

The key word in this phase of a program is *consistency*. Functionally, it ensures that the standards developed by the design consultant and management are systematically reproduced. The symbol or mark itself is often less important than its systematic implementation. Just as a good package cannot sell a bad product, a good mark inconsistently applied is actually less effective than a weaker one that is systematically applied to all corporate-related materials. A company that uses different type styles or letterhead layouts and maintains inconsistent color controls can only project a confusing and disorganized image to its various publics, regardless of how attractive the symbol may be.

WHAT SHOULD GO INTO THE MANUAL?

The information contained in a manual will depend in part on the needs and activities of a company. The following outline provides a sample listing of corporate-related materials used by many types of companies. It can serve as a reference for detailing a standards manual. However, the entries will vary according to the nature of the organization. For example, a fast-food franchise will have different needs from a pharmaceutical firm.

CORPORATE CHECKLIST

I. Introduction
   A. Table of contents
   B. Introductory letter/message from the president
   C. How to use the manual
   D. Basic terminology
   E. Symbol variations
   F. Symbol colors

G. Symbol color variations (color samples)
H. Consistent use of symbol (coordination of corporate identity)
I. Subsidiary signatures
J. Product signatures

2. Symbol
   A. Symbol variations—positive, negative, and screened
   B. Use of graphic elements
   C. Symbol arrangements (step-repeat pattern, three-dimensional, and so on)
   D. Reproduction of symbol (include do's and don'ts)
   E. Typography
   F. Compatible typography

3. Stationery
   A. General guidelines
      1. Paper stock
      2. Format
      3. Location of symbol
      4. Color
      5. Typography
   B. Executive letterhead
   C. Standard letterhead
   D. Executive business card
   E. Standard business card
   F. Executive envelope
   G. Standard #10 envelope
   H. Airmail envelope
   I. Window envelope
   J. Statement
   K. Mailing label
   L. Press release

M. Shipping envelope (various sizes)
N. Subsidiary letterhead
O. Subsidiary envelope
P. Subsidiary business card

4. Forms
   A. Guidelines
      1. Paper stock
      2. Format
      3. Color
      4. Typography
   B. Internal/external form
   C. Vertical grid
   D. Horizontal grid
   E. Reporting form
   F. Memorandum
   G. Purchase order
   H. Invoice
   I. Shipping form

5. Marketing and sales literature
   A. Annual reports
   B. Quarterly reports
   C. Brochures
   D. Company newsletters
   E. Invitation cards and envelopes
   F. Catalogs
   G. Tags and labels
   H. Direct mail pieces
   I. Merchandising aids
   J. Uniforms
   K. Point-of-purchase displays
   L. Exhibits
   M. Posters

6. Signage
   A. Guidelines for signage

1. Line of sight
2. Long-distance signing
3. Materials
4. Colors

B. Exterior signage
C. Interior signage
   1. directional
7. Transportation
   A. Service vehicles (vans, buses, automobiles)
   B. Trucks
   C. Company airplanes
   D. Freighters
   E. Tanker trucks
   F. Parking lot stickers
   G. Company flag
8. Packaging
   A. Guidelines
      1. Layout
      2. Product name
      3. Typography
      4. Color-coding system
      5. Legal considerations
      6. Sizes of packages and labels
   B. Cartons
   C. Paper bags
   D. Tubes
   E. Shipping containers
   F. Gift boxes
   G. Plastic bags
   H. Wrapping paper
   I. Wrapping tape
9. Other applications
   A. Nameplates
   B. Suitcase tags
   C. Employee pins
   D. Matches
   E. Gift ties
   F. Glasses
10. Technical supplement
    A. Guidelines
    B. Master artwork

Entries should be accompanied by a sample illustrating the text (where possible) and describing the proper use of the design—the size, position, color, and typography. The text should be simple and straightforward—not everyone using the manual will be in the graphics industry. Because of this, a glossary of basic terminology at the beginning of the manual is useful, as it will eliminate a lot of confusion regarding terms. The glossary should include some of the following terms:

Corporate identity. A desired image acquired and communicated by the company to the public through consistent visual communications.

Identity system. A system of visual communications, graphically coordinated in such a way that the public easily identifies the company and its activities.

Symbol. A graphic device (mark) that distinguishes a company, its activities, and its products and promotes immediate identification of these by the public.

Logotype. The company name, designed in a unique and individual form. This does not include setting the name in an existing type style.

Signature. The company name (logotype) and symbol used as a unit in a variety of arrangements that describe the company, its divisions, or its activities.

Corporate colors. Used wherever possible, the color combination chosen to represent the company.

Compatible typography. A type style that complements the signature used for supplementary copy, such as address blocks and advertisements.

Master artwork. A film negative or positive of approved signature arrangements (flush left, centered, flush right, negative, and so on). These films are available from the corporate identity coordinator and are used to make reproduction-quality photostats. *Master artwork alone should be used for reproduction.*

A manual should also include a table of contents or introductory headings to facilitate finding the material needed.

Most manuals begin with an introductory letter from the chief executive officer that explains and endorses the program. The success of any corporate identity program depends on the enthusiastic support of top-level management, and the introductory letter assures that the program is being taken seriously by everyone concerned. The letter should explain why the program was initiated and the importance of carrying out the program exactly as it was designed.

A person or department should be responsible for answering all questions about the manual. Although a designer may try to set guidelines for all aspects of a symbol's implementation, a corporate identity coordinator can assure the continuity of the symbol in unexpected instances. In larger organizations an entire department may be devoted to the program's implementation. Smaller companies may have an individual assigned to be the "keeper of the corporate identity keys." The titles may vary (corporate identity director, corporate communications officer, corporate identity coordinator), but the major responsibility is relatively the same—the administrator of the communications program.

Everyone involved in the advertising, promotion, public relations, purchasing, and production of the company symbol should have a copy of the manual. Sometimes copies are given to major suppliers, such as printers or packaging manufacturers. The corporate identity director should supervise the production of the items, so that if something does not comply with its use as specified in the manual, it can be adjusted immediately.

Implementing a program is not an overnight process. Priorities should be set for the identity program in the early phases of the project. Depending on the budget, a company may decide to print all of the materials outlined in the manual at once (a costly procedure) or to print them gradually, ordering materials with the new symbol only when supplies must be replaced. Replacing materials gradually can take anywhere from two to five years (depending on the company's supplies and resources) but is certainly more cost-effective. New companies can implement the identity program gradually by ordering materials as they are needed.

Although some corporations do not adopt a corporate identification program because of the expense, an identification system can substantially reduce printing costs and increase efficiency in purchasing. A major California bank saved over $300,000 during the first two years alone on printing just by standardizing its forms. By specifying paper stock, all purchasing can be done in volume, resulting in substantial long-term savings. The major savings comes from streamlining and standardizing all visual communications.

FORMAT

The manual should be thought of as an ongoing concept, so that when changes or additions are needed, they can easily be incorporated. Companies that are involved in mergers or acquisitions should have programs that are flexible enough to incorporate any new divisions, products, or companies. Because the manual should be adaptable, a binder is ideal; changes can be made quickly and inexpensively. Manuals that are bound together are obviously more difficult and costly to update. There is a disadvantage to using a loose-leaf binder, however—pages may disappear, and, over time, it may be forgotten that those particular guidelines were set. This is why a corporate identity

director is so important in maintaining strict controls.

LENGTH

The size of a standards manual can range from three photocopied pages to hundreds of pages bound in several volumes and reproduced in four colors with tip-ins of actual printed pieces. The length is governed by the materials required, the complexity of the program, and the budget allocated for the consultant's fees and production costs. If the budget is small, a minimanual can be produced in black-and-white to cover the major elements of the identity program and describe information needed to ensure proper reproduction of the symbol.

SEPARATE BUDGETS

Consultant fees for the corporate identity manual will vary, depending on the complexity of the manual and the consultant's experience. A manual is usually included in an identity proposal, but there are instances where a separate budget is needed (for example, when an existing symbol needs only slight modification). For a sample proposal see Appendix 5.

Fees can vary from $5,000 for a minimanual to $500,000 for a manual created for a multinational company.

A good designer may cost more, but he may end up saving a company money by avoiding costly printing mistakes and by setting up a program that makes the best possible impression on its various publics (fig. 8-1).

8-1. *Sample pages from the Apple Computer corporate identity manual.*

Everywhere in the world the Apple logo appears, it's our way of showing our true colors. It is extremely valuable to us—a reflection of Apple quality, Apple innovation, Apple reliability, Apple friendliness.

Enormous effort has gone into these **Corporate Identity Guidelines** to define and refine all the elements that make up Apple's unmistakable presence. We've included standards for everything from colors and sizes for the Apple logo to type styles, trademarks, and legal requirements.

We've worked hard to shape Apple's corporate identity, and we must work equally hard to protect what we've created. Make every effort, therefore, to follow these guidelines.

Thanks for your cooperation.

Creative Services Department
Cupertino, California

Contents

The Apple logo rendered in six colors is the corporate logo and registered trademark of Apple Computer. It is the primary link and support for all elements and expressions of Apple's Corporate Identity Program.

Because the logo has become virtually synonymous with Apple, the logo usually is the only signature required in order to identify the company. In those countries where Apple's logo is not widely recognized, the logotype should also be used. Please refer to the logotype and signature sections for guidance in use and placement of logotype.

Logo

A01.1

Logo
Solid

Logo
Keyline

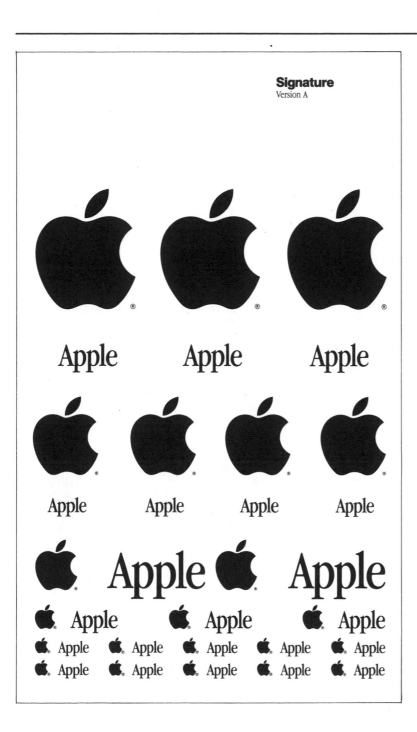

Signature
Version A

The Apple logo may be reversed to white from a dark background. The logo in reverse provides additional versatility, particularly in situations where a full-color treatment is not possible or economical. This rendition can only be used successfully, however, where the background offers sufficient contrast to allow the Apple logo to be clearly perceived. The gray background used in the illustration on this page provides the minimum contrast allowed. Lighter backgrounds are not acceptable, because detail and readability are lost.

Logo
Reversed to White

Apple Gray

A05.1

The Apple logotype, incorporating Apple's corporate trade name—Apple Computer, Inc., is composed of unique letterforms derived from the ITC Garamond type-style family, expressly for use by Apple. The logotype is the only letterform and type configuration that can be used where a legal corporate signature is required.

The Apple logotype is second only to the Apple logo as the major visual identifier of Apple Computer. Together, these two elements compose the corporate signature.

Because the logotype is the text element of the Apple identity and Apple signature, it is legally protected—just as the Apple logo is protected. Its protectability is based on its unique design; therefore, the logotype and its letterforms must never be altered or reproportioned in any way.

The logotype is always presented in black, Apple Gray, or in reverse to white. It is never printed in other colors.

Logotype art is provided in the reproduction art section of these guidelines.

Logotype
Corporate

Apple Computer, Inc.

The logotypes used to identify various products are illustrated below. The product logotypes are a derivation of the ITC Garamond type style family. It is a light, condensed version that resembles and is compatible with the corporate logotype.

Art for all product logotypes is provided in the reproduction art section of these guidelines and should be used whenever the logotypes are to be produced. Replacement art is available from the Creative Services Department.

Logotypes
Product

Macintosh™

Apple® IIe

Apple® IIc

Signature staging follows the rules established for staging of the logo. As is illustrated here, the minimum clear space required on all sides of the signature is X—where X equals the proportional width established for the logo. Note that the signature is positioned a minimum space of X in from the near side of the presentation piece or document, and is a minimum space of X down from the top or up from the bottom.

Art is provided in the reproduction art section of these guidelines and should be used whenever the logotypes are to be produced. Replacement art is available from the Creative Services Department.

Shown in the three variations below, are examples of how the legal signature should be used on the back of literature.

Version A shows the back of a standard brochure with the logo placed at the top left corner with the logotype and address at the bottom left corner.

Version B shows logo, logotype and address combined at the bottom left corner.

Version C shows placement when more than one address is used.

Signature
Staging

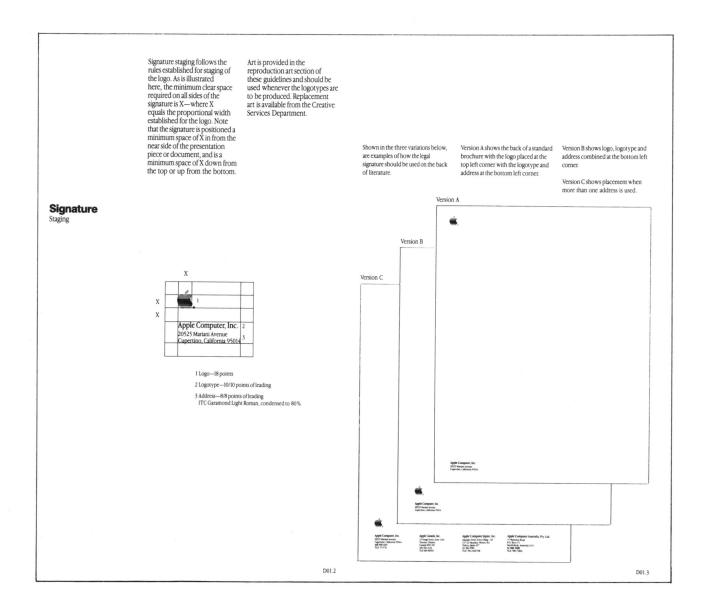

1 Logo—18 points

2 Logotype—10/10 points of leading

3 Address—8/8 points of leading
ITC Garamond Light Roman, condensed to 80%

D01.2

D01.3

The ITC Garamond type-style family is the preferred type style for primary use. The ITC Garamond variations that are recommended for use are illustrated here and on the adjoining pages.

Type Style
Primary Usage

ITC Garamond Light Roman, condensed to 80% of Roman

A B C D E F G H I J K L M
N O P Q R S T U V W X Y Z
a b c d e f g h i j k l m n o
p q r s t u v w x y z

ITC Garamond Book Roman, condensed to 80% of Roman

A B C D E F G H I J K L M
N O P Q R S T U V W X Y Z
a b c d e f g h i j k l m n o
p q r s t u v w x y z

ITC Garamond Bold Roman, condensed to 75% of Roman

A B C D E F G H I J K L M
N O P Q R S T U V W X Y Z
a b c d e f g h i j k l m n o
p q r s t u v w x y z

E01.1

The Helvetica type-style family has been selected as most suitable for secondary usage because it visually complements the logotype and the ITC Garamond typefaces preferred for primary usage.

Type Style
Secondary Usage

Helvetica Light

ABCDEFGHIJKLM
NOPQRSTUVWXYZ
abcdefghijklmno
pqrstuvwxyz

Helvetica Regular

ABCDEFGHIJKLM
NOPQRSTUVWXYZ
abcdefghijklmno
pqrstuvwxyz

Helvetica Bold

**ABCDEFGHIJKLM
NOPQRSTUVWXYZ
abcdefghijklmno
pqrstuvwxyz**

E02.1

Corporate business cards are intended as official introductions of Apple personnel. The cards provide a prime opportunity to communicate the Apple identity. For that reason, Apple business cards are designed to achieve the important Apple identity goals.

Be certain that all business cards produced for Apple conform to the examples shown and described in this section.

The version of the corporate business card shown here is the only configuration approved for use in the U.S. No other variations should be developed without the express approval of the Creative Services Department.

Art for all elements of the Apple business card is provided in the reproduction art section. The reproduction art is camera-ready and should be used whenever business cards are to be produced. Replacement art is available from the Creative Services Department.

Business Cards
Standard

Size: 3½ x 2 inches

Note: All measurements below are given in picas.

A = 5.25
B = 3.

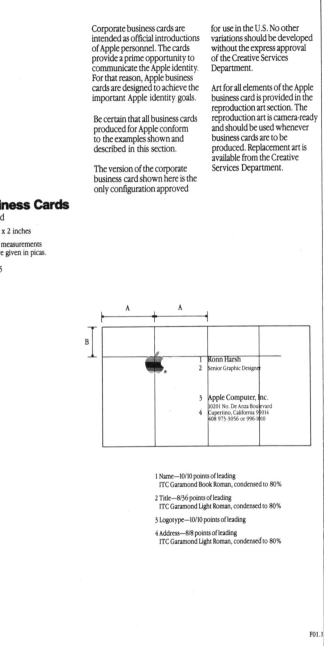

1 Name—10/10 points of leading
  ITC Garamond Book Roman, condensed to 80%

2 Title—8/36 points of leading
  ITC Garamond Light Roman, condensed to 80%

3 Logotype—10/10 points of leading

4 Address—8/8 points of leading
  ITC Garamond Light Roman, condensed to 80%

F01.1

Like business cards, the letterhead presents the Apple identity. People who receive letters from Apple should also receive a strong and positive visual message from the stationery itself.

In order to derive maximum identity advantage from each written business communication, it is essential that the corporate letterhead conform to the example shown here—it must not be altered or redesigned in any way.

Art for all elements of the Apple corporate letterhead is provided in the reproduction art section. The reproduction art is camera-ready and should be used whenever letterheads are to be produced. Replacement art is available from the Creative Services Department.

Letterhead
Corporate

1 Logo—18 points

2 Logotype—10/10 points of leading

3 Address—8/8 points of leading
   ITC Garamond Light Roman, condensed to 80%

 1

Apple Computer, Inc. 2
20525 Mariani Avenue
Cupertino, California 95014 3

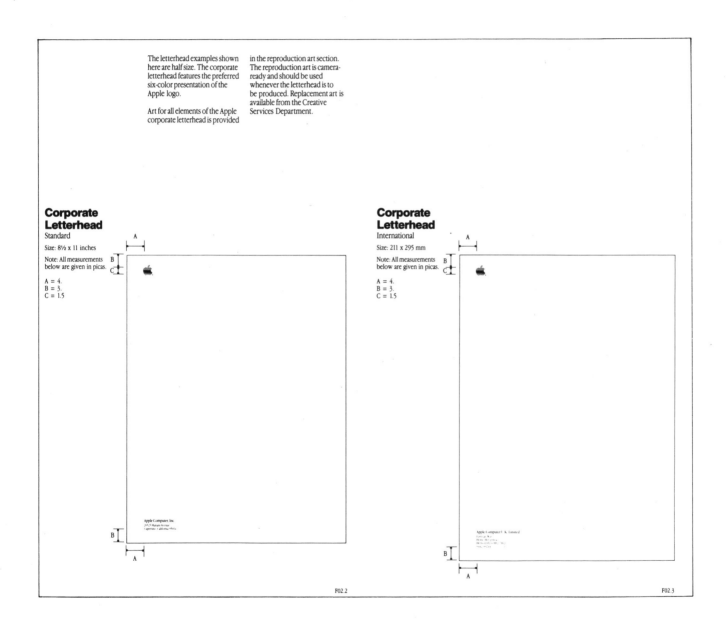

The letterhead examples shown here are half size. The corporate letterhead features the preferred six-color presentation of the Apple logo.

Art for all elements of the Apple corporate letterhead is provided in the reproduction art section. The reproduction art is camera-ready and should be used whenever the letterhead is to be produced. Replacement art is available from the Creative Services Department.

Corporate Letterhead
Standard

Size: 8½ x 11 inches

Note: All measurements below are given in picas.

A = 4.
B = 3.
C = 1.5

A
B
C

Apple Computer, Inc.
20525 Mariani Avenue
Cupertino, California 95014

B

A

F02.2

Corporate Letterhead
International

Size: 211 x 295 mm

Note: All measurements below are given in picas.

A = 4.
B = 3.
C = 1.5

A
B
C

Apple Computer UK, Limited
Eastman Way
Hemel Hempstead
Hertfordshire HP2 7HQ
England

B

A

F02.3

Another important component of corporate stationery, envelopes also present the Apple identity to a large audience. Anyone receiving mail from Apple should receive from the envelope a strong, positive visual presentation of the Apple identity.

The envelopes described on the following pages are designed to do just that—establish strong visual recognition of the Apple identity. It is important, therefore, that the envelope design be just as described, and not be altered or redesigned in any way.

The envelopes illustrated on these pages are shown at 50% of the actual envelope size.

Art for all elements is provided in the reproduction art section. The reproduction art is camera-ready and should be used whenever envelopes are to be produced. Replacement art is available from the Creative Services Department.

Envelopes
Standard

Size: 9½ x 4⅛ inches

Note: All measurements below are given in picas.

A = 4.
B = 3.
C = 1.5

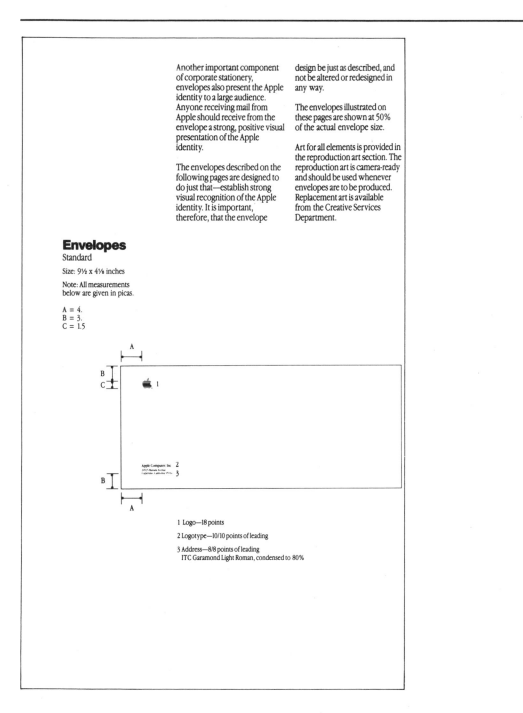

1 Logo—18 points

2 Logotype—10/10 points of leading

3 Address—8/8 points of leading
ITC Garamond Light Roman, condensed to 80%

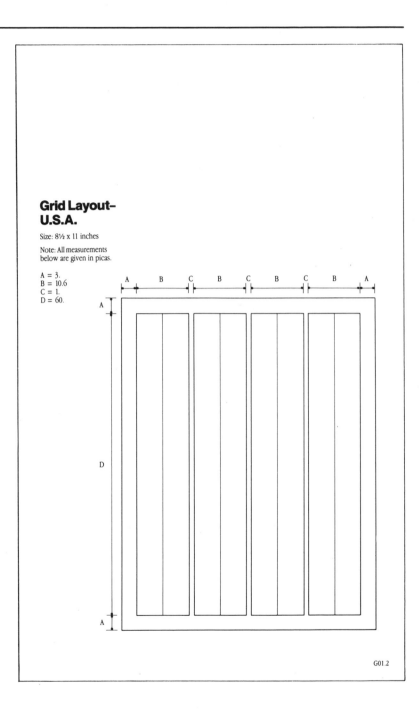

**Grid Layout–
U.S.A.**

Size: 8½ x 11 inches

Note: All measurements
below are given in picas.

A = 3.
B = 10.6
C = 1.
D = 60.

G01.2

9 WHAT IS IN A NAME?

In today's competitive marketplace, a name can determine whether or not a company succeeds in creating a lasting impression. Unfortunately, no one gets a second chance to make a first impression. Just as a person's name can affect his life, a bad or inappropriate name can create an undesirable image for a company.

The following are examples of inappropriate names:

• General Motors: One of the giants of American industry used as its corporate tag line, "Body by Fisher." Translated to Flemish, this means "Corpse by Fisher."

• Colgate-Palmolive: The company introduced CUE toothpaste in France, completely unaware that the word *cue* referred to a part of the anatomy that definitely did not relate to brushing teeth.

• Chevrolet: This time General Motors had to change the name under which "Nova" was marketed in Puerto Rico after realizing that *no va* means "it does not run" in Spanish.

Many of the old familiar names were derived from family surnames—Ford, Kraft, and DuPont all looked to their heritage for assistance. Because of the increased numbers of products and companies today, new name strategies work better. Just as an identity should visually grab the consumer, the name should tell almost immediately what the product's or company's major benefit is—Head & Shoulders, MicroPro, DieHard batteries.

REASONS FOR A NAME CHANGE

A name change can be a time-consuming and expensive undertaking. The long-term results, however, of an inappropriate name can be far more expensive. Reasons for change might be that the present company name is:

• Misleading: Efforts to present a broad-based appeal or extend the product line are restrained by a one-product image; American Can Company became Primerica; Hershey Chocolate became Hershey Foods.

• Too long: Olin Matheson Chemical Corporation was changed to Olin.

• Out of date: An old-fashioned image was thought to be turning off potential consumers, so American Brake and Shoe Foundry Company became ABEX.

• Inappropriate for multinational growth: U.S. Rubber became UNIROYAL.

• Geographically restrictive: Nebraska Consolidated Mills Company became ConAgra; Allegheny Airlines became USAir; Minnesota Mining & Manufacturing became the 3M Company.

• Not memorable: City Services Oil Company became CITGO.

• Opportunities presented by mergers or acquisitions: When two or more firms merge, the newly acquired company often wants to capitalize on the parent company's reputation. Acquired by the Bank of America, General Acceptance Corporation became Finance America.

• Bad for public relations: R.J. Reynold Tobacco Company became R.J. Reynolds Industries; American Tobacco Company became American Brands.

Before the decision to create a new name is made, the consultant should work with the client to:

1. **Establish objective and criteria.** Just as objectives must be determined before creating a new identity, a new name should satisfy specific goals.

2. **Weigh the assets and liabilities of the present name.** Equities established in a company's name are sometimes the strongest element of the corporation's identity.

3. **Consider long-range goals.** Where is the company likely to be in ten, twenty, or thirty years. Will the name still be appropriate at that time?

4. **Consider the target market.** Who is going to use the name? How easy is it going to be to pronounce? Is the target audience local, regional, national, or international?

BASIC NAME CATEGORIES

Descriptive names conjure up images that are either directly or indirectly related to the product or company. These types of names sometimes go over the edge by being too restrictive. For example, when individuals who fly frequently were surveyed, more than 25 percent of them stated they would avoid Allegheny Airlines (even though it was the sixth largest passenger airline in the United States at the time), because they preferred a national over a regional airline. Its regional name placed Allegheny in a different category from airlines such as United and American. As a result of the survey, Allegheny changed its name to USAir; in 1982 it had the largest net profit of any airline in the world.

A company name in the form of initials—IBM, RCA, GE, IT&T—is effective if the company has years of proven service. Using initials to name a new company, however, could have disastrous results, as initials tend to be neither memorable nor evocative.

Abstract or coined names are those that are made up and initially mean nothing to the consumer. Kodak, Xerox, and Kotex are all examples of coined words. The advantages of creating a coined word is the good chance that it will be legally available. The disadvantage is that in order to make a "nothing name" mean something to the consumer, the company must launch a massive campaign to introduce and anchor the name in the mind of the consumer.

DEVELOPING NAMES: THE CREATIVE PROCESS

Developing names does not differ drastically from the process of creating visual identities; it is an inventive and imaginative function that uses similar faculties. Because of this, the identity consultant's domain has broadened to include naming studies.

Certain readily available resources are invaluable. Dictionaries—Spanish, French, Latin, and English—can be a tremendous source for generating roots, prefixes, and suffixes. A thesaurus is a useful tool for manipulating and creating "action" words that help stimulate the mind. A person can take the objectives he is working on and think of them in terms of different words. By doing this, he can see the word list grow, which gets the mind stimulated and ready for action.

Books of quotations and slang are also useful creative tools, as are magazines and specialty books.

There are two methods of creating a naming program: brainstorming and computer generation.

BRAINSTORMING

Naming sessions usually involve a small group of people—anywhere from two to ten—with varied backgrounds and different perspectives. Participants, however, must be bright, creative people with rich vocabularies. A typical session might include an electrical engineer, a writer, a marketing researcher, a designer, and an opera singer.

The moderator, or leader, of these sessions has the responsibility of preparing a small brief that describes the company, its objectives, and the naming criteria by which the favored names are to be later evaluated. Then he must lead the group in exchanging ideas that stimulate concepts in the minds of others, because, after about fifteen to twenty minutes of trying to think of a name, people get bogged down. Someone has to prod them to keep them going, and creating names is not easy work. He might, for example, keep up continuous suggestions of words that will suggest new words and word combinations.

All names and ideas should either be written on a blackboard or a large sheet of paper so that everyone in the room can see them.

In the process of developing names the consultant may find that the best ideas do not come in the sessions, but as a delayed result of them, while eating, driving down the highway, or working on another assignment. This is because the subconscious is constantly working on problems, and when one least expects it, that great name can surface.

COMPUTER GENERATION

Most recently, a computer software program, Namer by Salinon, was introduced on the market. A powerful tool for generating names, it offers techniques and features that are unavailable from any other source. It is easy to use and allows the operator to specify the type of name for which he is looking.

This program satisfies four common types of naming needs:

• The Original Name Generator: This builds names with no input required from the user. It uses conditional probabilities and linguistic algorithms based on studies of tens of thousands of English words and names. The names generated are totally unknown but usually sound like words derived from the English language (Zipad, Corloon).

• The Connotation Synthesizer: This combines morphemes, phrases, and syllables with explicit or implied meanings. The operator selects the desired connotations for the name, and the system accesses its data base of word parts with those meanings to create a new name. The user can also create his own data base of phrases or syllables. In this case, the root parts are combined to derive new words that convey the image desired for the company, product, or service (AquaFlow, AutoDoc).

• The Adaptive Learning Method: This allows the operator to control virtually every element in the formation of new names. It provides control over the starting, middle, and ending letter pairs; fixed characters at the beginning and the end of the name; the length of the name; and number and placement of vow-

els and consonants in the name. It then generates names with those characteristics and asks the operator to rate the name on a scale from one to nine. Based on the name ratings, this method automatically adapts or modifies its name-generating tables and rules to create names more in line with what the operator desires. This method requires more input from the user.

• The Phrase Maker: This creates names, slogans, and acronyms by combining words into phrases. It allows the operator to select synonyms from its dictionary, to enter and store his own words, and to specify the combination order used to generate new names. It is fairly easy to use and the names it generates usually have a specific meaning, since they are composed of complete words (Crunchy Mint Cookies, Sam's Superior Athletic Warehouse).

The program is also equipped with a screening mechanism that checks new names for possible off-color or vulgar meanings in five languages—English, Spanish, Italian, German, and French. The operator enters the name to be checked; the system responds with the sound of a siren if a match is found in its coded data base. Operators are not told the meaning of the word but are told which language is involved.

The program is an easy-to-use system for naming things and is the first of its kind on the marketplace. Namer is available from Salinon Corporation, 7430 Greenville Ave., Dallas, TX 75231.

EVALUATING NAMES

After the list has been generated, the names are scanned individually by the same naming group used in the brainstorming session and selected for their appropriateness. The group should then choose 50 to 100 of their favorite names. The selection process then becomes narrower, as the names are judged against the criteria established earlier. When evaluating names certain things should be kept in mind in addition to those set objectives:

- Is the name memorable, unique, and distinctive?
- Does it describe the product, service, or company?
- Is it easy to remember? Is it catchy or a play on words?
- Will it create a favorable impression on the target market?
- Does it have strong promotional capacity? Product line extension? Possibilities for graphic extension?

The lists of names are then narrowed down to a handful of favorites. Each person on the team rates each name on a point system. These are evaluated individually on a scale of: Very Strong +2, Strong +1, Somewhat Weak −1, and Weak −2. A total score is then arrived at for each of the names in the final running. The favored names are then tested with qualified consumers (with regard to demographics and psychographics), who are asked to give an opinion about them and to make a choice among names. The process of evaluating the individual names on the list that is generated is done by the creative team or the naming group, not the intended target market. Participants in the market study will usually give opinions for three to five of the favored names. Verbal tests are usually conducted with the marketing research participants, such as focus group discussions or interviews. The following is an outline of a general testing technique:

1. The individual interviewed is shown one of the favored names on a card and asked to free-associate. What does it make him think of? What kind of image does it create? Ultimately, what does it mean to him?

2. The participant is asked, if this were the name of a company, what would its products be? What type of company would it not be? What type of company would it be to work for?

3. He is then asked which of the names he best recalls and why.

At this point, designers should take the favored names and begin preliminary conceptual sketches to accompany the names, and they should begin to explore the possible graphic value of each.

LEGAL AVAILABILITY OF TRADEMARKS AND TRADE NAMES
REGISTERING A TRADEMARK

Most people are not familiar with the process for registering a trademark and its legal implications. A trademark is a word, name, symbol, device, or any combination of these used by a manufacturer or merchant to identify his products and distinguish them from the competition. A trademark is not only used to distinguish one manufacturer's goods from those of another but also to indicate to purchasers that the quality of the products bearing the mark remains the same. A trademark identifies a product; a trade name is used to identify a producer.

The rights to a trademark are established by actual use of the mark on goods "moving in trade"; use must continue for the rights to the mark to be maintained. No rights are established until there has been actual use, and a trademark cannot be registered until the goods bearing the mark have been sold or shipped in interstate, foreign, or territorial commerce.

Trademark rights are protected under common law; it is not "technically" necessary for the trademark owner to register his mark. However, a common law marriage, for example, is much harder to authenticate than a "legal paper marriage." Registration of the trademark can result in material advantages to the trademark owner, as it gives notice of his claim of ownership, bolsters his exclusive right to use the mark on the goods cited in the registration, and establishes the date that the mark officially became his.

The importance of registering a trademark is illustrated by the following anecdote from Alan Fletcher's book *Living By Design*:

Unable to maintain the exclusivity of the word "Cola," the Coca Cola Company undertook a worldwide programme to shorten their name to the colloquial "Coke." Instructions were given to register this name, and a company director in South America, who was a little slow off the mark, arrived at the appropriate registration office only to find an unscrupulous employee had got there first. They had to pay him a half a million pounds to buy back the name!

The U.S. Patent and Trademark Office has jurisdiction over all federal registrations. Therefore, if the product or services are being marketed on an interstate level, a federal registration is appropriate. If the merchant is involved in intrastate commerce only, then the mark can be registered in the state where the product or service is sold. When goods or services are sold or shipped internationally, a registration must be obtained in each country in which the protection is desired. A U.S. registration may in fact be used as the basis for obtaining registration in a number of countries.

In order to qualify for registration with the U.S. Patent and Trademark Office, the following must be submitted:

- a written application properly notarized
- a drawing of the mark
- five samples of the mark as it is actually being used
- the filing fee

The registration is good for twenty years from the date of issue, and it may be renewed at the end of that time period, as long as it is still being used in commerce. There are different ways to indicate that a trademark is actually registered: by using the words "Registered in U.S. Patent Office" or the abbreviation "Reg. U.S. Patent Office" or by using an ®. Any of these should be placed as close to the actual trademark as possible. It is illegal to use these indications before the registration is complete. Indications such as "TM" or "Trademark," placed as close as possible to the actual trademark, are used to convey that the company intends to register the mark or that it considers the mark its property under common law.

There are several publications on the subject available from the U.S. Patent and Trademark Office. For further information and a list of publications, write to U.S. Department of Commerce, Patent and Trademark Office, Washington, DC 20231.

APPENDIX 1
SAMPLE PROPOSAL

PHASE I

In Phase I the objective will be to understand each aspect of Widget Corporation's current identity situation thoroughly. A set of communications objectives will be prepared that will address each of these separately. Alternative strategic positionings will be developed for the company; these will then be realized with a design. At the end of Phase I, we will present ideas for discussion and consideration at a work session attended by Widget's management team and ours. Phase I will be conducted as follows:

A. BRIEFING SESSION

After we receive authorization to proceed, we will spend several days at Widget headquarters to be briefed on all aspects of the program from management's viewpoint. We will be particularly interested in reviewing any relevant material and data that is available and in talking with key management at Widget's headquarters. We will also visit the following regional offices: New York, Chicago, Los Angeles, Boston, Atlanta, Dallas, and San Francisco. The primary purpose of these sessions will be to examine all pertinent information and to help us determine the direction that the

program will take during the graphic development stages.

B. MANAGEMENT INTERVIEWS

In-depth interviews with ten to twelve of Widget's key managers will be conducted to gain a thorough understanding of their marketing and communication requirements. We expect that this will include members of the top management group, marketing directors, and anyone else thought to be appropriate. This will help us gain diverse opinions and ideas concerning Widget's present and future marketing and communication goals.

C. FACILITIES AUDIT

Members of our consulting team will visit selected Widget stores in major cities. The aim will be to audit the existing communications situation and to conduct informal interviews with local personnel (if authorized by Widget) in order to gain insight into their view of the company's identity, as it is now and as they think it ought to be.

An important function of this field audit will be the compilation of a photographic record of actual conditions. Visual materials of this type, together with other visual references provided by Widget, will be used extensively in the briefing of the design team and will have a bearing on the design problems at hand.

D. REVIEW EXISTING DATA AND RESEARCH

We will determine what information is available and appropriate for consideration. This information should relate to how Widget and Widget competitors are currently perceived.

E. VISUAL AUDIT

An important ingredient in our conceptual and creative problem-solving methods as designers is to understand the environment—external and internal—in which the design and the subsequent communications system must work. The team will visit, photograph, and analyze Widget's regional offices, plus three to four principal competitive offices. We will also audit a selection of printed items with Widget's current identity: letterhead, forms, business cards, brochures, etc.

F. PRESENTATION TO MANAGEMENT

Phase I will conclude with an informal presentation to Widget management at its headquarters, during which we will summarize our findings, conclusions, and recommendations. Specific recommendations for a systems approach to identity development will be offered, and with management's agreement on the objectives identified, we will expect approval to proceed to the next phase—design exploration.

PHASE II— DESIGN EXPLORATION

The process of creative design development now begins. The purpose of this second phase is to develop alternative design systems in prototypical form, as follows:

A. GRAPHIC EXPLORATION

A team of designers will begin to explore graphic expressions of the chosen communications objectives. Typically, this exploration will result in a broad range of graphic directions. Having thoroughly explored those basic concepts, we will work on those visual elements that will form the basis upon which the communications system will depend:

1. The logotype: the distinctive characterization of the Widget signature and Widget's other group companies and products.

2. The symbol: by itself or in combination with the logotype.

3. Corporate colors: combinations of different color schemes will be explored.

Through a series of critiques and meetings, the three most appropriate graphic directions will be selected for prototypical development. However, at the presentation at the end of this phase, all work done to date will be shown to Widget management.

B. PROTOTYPICAL DEVELOPMENT

The graphic directions selected will be applied systematically to three or four prototype usages. These will come from different areas of Widget's operations, so that we can clearly demonstrate the validity of each approach. This helps us further explore and understand the strengths and weaknesses of each graphic approach and how to improve them. We will produce four prototypical items:

1. a letterhead
2. an exterior sign in two-dimensional format
3. a consumer product
4. an existing collateral piece modified to incorporate the new corporate symbol

C. WORK SESSION

Phase II will conclude with a presentation to management reviewing all work done but focusing on the prototype design systems for the two to three best graphic directions. With Widget's participation and agreement, we will then discuss and decide which design direction will be adopted for Widget's new identity.

PHASE III— DESIGN REFINEMENT

At this stage, we will proceed to the refinement and modification of the system agreed upon at the last work session. We will, in addition, extend the refined graphic system to the existing prototypes. This will substantially aid Widget in visualizing the comprehensive application of the design system.

A. DESIGN REFINEMENT

The selected identity system will be fully refined, accommodating any agreed changes. Basic guidelines will be established for systematic usage.

B. DESIGN EXTENSION

We will then graphically extend the new concept onto the same four areas of usage (see Phase IIB).

C. PRESENTATION TO MANAGEMENT

Having completed the modification and refinement of the preferred direction, we will demonstrate the system, discuss the advantages and opportunities in the approach, and recommend a final approach. At the end of this presentation, we would expect to obtain approval and acceptance of the system recommended as well as permission to proceed to Phase IV.

PHASE IV— IMPLEMENTATION

Implementation refers to the application of the accepted design system throughout Widget's organization. We will prepare a graphics standards manual to ensure that deviations of the symbol and its application do not occur. (See separate sample proposal for a graphic standards manual in Appendix 5.)

BUDGET AND TIME CONSIDERATIONS

Phase I—Analysis
A. Briefing Sessions
B. Management Interviews
C. Facilities Audit
D. Review Existing Data and Research
E. Conduct Visual Audit
F. Presentation to Management
Time: X–XX weeks; **Budget**: $XX,XXX

Phase II—Design Exploration
A. Graphic Exploration
B. Prototypical Development
C. Work Session
Time: X–XX weeks; **Budget**: $XX,XXX

Phase III—Design Refinement
A. Refinement
B. Design Extension
C. Presentation to Management
Time: X–XX weeks; **Budget**: $XX,XXX

Phase IV—Implementation
A. Development of a Graphics Manual
Time: XX weeks; **Budget**: $XXX,XXX

Total Budget and Time: XX–XXX weeks, $XXX,XXX

APPENDIX 2
SAMPLE QUESTIONNAIRE

Name:_____

Title:_____

Responsibilities:_____

Length of time in this position:_____

Purpose of the interview:

As you have been informed, Napoles Associates has been retained to conduct a study and analysis of Widget's image in various key markets. The image of Widget Corporation (the way in which the company is perceived by consumers, customers, and various other publics) is linked with the Widget products themselves. Of course, your opinions will remain anonymous and confidential and will be added to others to analyze overall patterns of Widget's image and status.

1. Describe your position in the organization. Perhaps you could give me an organizational chart of your firm indicating your department in relation to the rest of the company.

2. In general, how do you feel about Widget's overall reputation?

3. What image should Widget and Widget products communicate and to whom?

4. With which public is it most important to develop a strong image? Please rank in order of importance—1 being most important and 5 being the least important.

_____consumers (retail)

_____distributors

_____the scientific community

_____government

_____financial institutions

5. How would you want your target public to describe Widget?

6. What are the major strengths of Widget?

7. What are the major weaknesses of Widget?

8. How would you like to see Widget products distributed and marketed?

9. Would there ever be a point at which the corporation would subordinate itself visually to the individual brands?

10. Do you feel that the present brand/product identities project the image you want them to? If so, how has it succeeded? If not, how has it fallen short of communication objectives?

11. What qualities should Widget Corporation convey?

12. Which of these qualities is most important?

13. What kinds of images do you think should be explored?

14. Here are some variations of the current Widget symbol (show card). In your opinion what are the positive aspects of the current Widget trademark? Do you think it will be effective in years to come? Should it be retained as is? Should it be modified or modernized in some way?

15. Where do you see the greatest opportunities for growth in your market?

16. In what way do you think changes in the Widget Corporation image might help you to realize these growth opportunities? In what ways might a change be harmful? What kinds of changes should be avoided?

17. Have you detected any changes in consumer habits during the course of your employment with Widget? Is the typical consumer getting older or younger? Are Widget products moving up or down on the economic scale? Are young people moving toward or away from Widget products? Are new products needed to meet the requirements of the youth market?

18. What are the differences in the marketing strategies of Widget's competition?

19. What do you consider to be the most immediate threat to the overall Widget image? Where do you see the business, say, ten years from now?

APPENDIX 3
SAMPLE DESIGN BRIEF

The Bank of California and the California National Bank have merged. After an extensive naming study, they decided to adopt the name MERIDIAN (according to the dictionary, meridian means the "highest point, culmination; one of the imaginary circles on the earth's surface passing through the north and south poles of any particular place"), because, although both banks were of the same size and have been operating for the same period of time (fifteen years), each name was too geographically restrictive. The total amount of deposits between the two banks exceeds $18,000,000. Their marketing objective for the upcoming year is to provide a full spectrum of competitive financial services in both the retail and corporate marketplace. Because of this, they have substantially increased the number of jointly participated activities and have focused their areas of expertise in such special areas as energy, natural resources, and technology.

Their plans for the future are to start new subsidiaries (primarily for the small- and medium-sized business) and establish core deposits that provide low-cost funds. (See attached annual report and relevant articles about the banks for further background and information.)

After completing the Phase I analysis, we have come up with the following observations and recommendations:

- The present identities, although well established, are not widely recognized.
- Neither of the two logotypes is distinctive.
- Major competition is adopting contemporary graphic treatments, and this trend will probably affect a great portion of California's banking and financial community.
- Meridian must develop a unique graphic style to compete with the larger banks.
- Meridian does not want to appear regional (i.e., northern California).
- Meridian must make the most of its limited budget for promotion.
- Meridian should appear modern and innovative and should cater to the small depositer, the middle-income patron, and corporate clients.
- Emphasis should be placed on a personal approach to banking ("We're not too big or too busy to help").
- The symbol should serve promotional needs and extend across a full range of banking products and services.
- Meridian's main objective is to provide a

full spectrum of competitive financial services in both the retail and corporate marketplaces.

• Meridian's symbol must work regionally and nationally to accommodate plans for aggressive expansion.

• Meridian's symbol should also communicate a friendly, warm bank, capitalizing on the bureaucratic image of larger competitive banks.

TECHNICAL REQUIREMENTS

The new image should provide consistent day and night visibility, as exterior signs will be one of the major vehicles for communication. The areas of design activity should encompass:

- symbol
- logotype
- colors
- primary signage
- advertising signatures
- checks and forms
- stationery items

Based on these objectives, you are to explore designs in two general directions: a contemporary symbol and logotype that suggest flexibility and innovation, a forward-looking, technically sophisticated organization that stresses progressive action; a traditional symbol and logotype that creates the impression of a solid, rather established, healthy bank— stable and conservative, rather than exciting.

Compare your preferred symbols with others in the banking industry. Please bring all tissues of creative exploration to the critique.

APPENDIX 4
COLOR ASSOCIATIONS

Red

Positive associations: happiness, aggression, impulsiveness, optimism, strength, masculinity, dynamism, mobility, passion; appeals to people who live their lives with a tremendous amount of intensity.

Negative associations: explosiveness, death, war, anarchy, the devil, blood.

Taste: flavorful, ripe, sweet

Language: red letter day (memorable), red in the face (anger), red tape (bureaucracy), in the red (debt), reds (communists)

Physical effects: warmth; it quickens the heart rate slightly and releases adrenalin into the bloodstream

Orange

Positive associations: communication, marriage (combination of red and yellow), organic, ambition, cheerfulness, expansiveness, richness, generosity, receptivity

Negative associations: malevolence

Taste: peppery, spicy, or orange flavored

Physical effects: warmth; resembles the light of a fireplace or a baker's oven

Yellow

Positive associations: cheeriness, enlightenment, sunshine, intelligence, action, youth

Negative associations: cowardliness, treachery

Taste: lemon, lightness, acidic

Language: yellow stripe (cowardliness), yellow journalism (sensationalism)

Physical effects: uplifting

Green

Positive associations: nature, fertility, life, hope, prosperity, stability, security (most nations have green currency)

Negative associations: decay, mold, envy, jealousy

Taste: fresh, slightly spicy, pine, lemon-lime

Language: green with envy, green (inexperienced; immature), greenbacks

Physical effects: calming, quieting

Blue

Positive associations: spirituality, femininity, conservatism, devotion, justice, rationality, passivism, tranquility, contentment, hygiene

Negative associations: melancholy, darkness, discouragement, doubt

Taste: berry flavor, sweet

Language: blue blood (nobility), blue mood (depression)

Physical effects: cool, soothing, restful

Purple

Positive associations: royalty, loyalty, power, memories, truth, religion

Negative associations: lust, decadence, penitence, mourning, secrecy, mystery

Taste: grape flavored

Physical effects: lilac (evokes feelings of fantasy)

Brown

Positive associations: organic, strength, masculinity, earthiness, compactness, health, utility

Negative associations: vulgarity, barrenness, impoverishment

Taste: suggestive of strong flavor (heavy and substantial); golden brown is appetizing (reminds people of roasting or baking, cereals, breads, or nuts)

Physical effects: lighter shades evoke feelings of health and well-being

Black

Positive associations: impenetrability, distinction, nobility, elegance, darkness

Negative associations: death, sickness, despair, denial, eternal silence, evil, sin

Taste: rich (represents the ultimate surrender)

Language: blackball, black market, blackmail, black sheep

White

Positive associations: purity, refreshment, perfection, infinite wisdom, truth

Negative associations: blankness, absolute silence, ghostliness, void

Taste: light, refined, delicate

Language: white flag (surrender, peace, truce)

Gray

Positive associations: autonomy, neutrality

Negative associations: indecision, fear, monotony, depression, age

Physical effects: coldness, dirt

APPENDIX 5
SAMPLE PROPOSAL FOR
GRAPHIC STANDARDS MANUAL

PHASE I— GRAPHIC STANDARDS MANUAL

The work covered in this phase includes the design of the manual, writing of the copy, and preparation of a comprehensive mock-up to illustrate the final appearance of the manual. In addition to containing all of the rules and guidelines, the manual serves as an example of the quality expected in all implementations of the Fireman's Fund identity.

Each section of the manual will have descriptive text and samples illustrating the rules and standards. Depending on the method of printing and binding, a flexible system can be set up that allows for additions or replacement(s) of inserts and sections as needed without the expense of redoing the entire system.

It is recommended that a letter be prepared for the President's signature, stating his endorsement of the program and stressing strict adherence to the rules and guidelines contained in the manual. This letter should be the first page of the manual. Contents for the proposed manual are as follows:

Introduction
A. Message from the President
B. Purpose and use of the manual

Section I—Primary Identity Elements
A. Symbol and logotype—relationship of trademark to logotype
B. Identity System—an identity system should be established that visually communicates its role and relationship to its parent, its divisions, and its products.
   1. Fireman's Fund symbol and logotype
   2. Fireman's Fund symbol and logotype coupled with the American Express symbol and tie-line
   3. Fireman's Fund and its relationship to its divisions
   4. Product lines and graphics with corporate linking phrase
C. Symbol Arrangements
   1. Signature requirements and guidelines
      a. Flush-left, flush-right, centered, positive, and negative versions
   2. Color standards guidelines (for Fireman's Fund symbol and American Express endorsement and tie-line)

a. Signature color variations and ink guidelines
   1. One color
   2. Two colors
   3. Three colors
   4. Foil hot-stamp
   5. Blind embossed symbol(s), with logotype in color
3. Typography—compatible family of type

Section II—Stationery Guidelines
A. Fireman's Fund corporate letterhead
  1. Standard letterhead
  2. Standard second sheet
  3. Executive letterhead
  4. Executive monarch
B. Fireman's Fund corporate envelopes
  1. 1.Standard # envelope
    2.Executive #10 envelope
    3.Monarch executive
    4.Standard # 11 manila
    5.Window envelope
    6.Standard #10 business reply
    7.Standard 9 × 12 and mailing label
C. Fireman's Fund business cards
  1. Standard business card
  2. Executive business card

Section III—Business Forms Guidelines
A. Press release, news item
B. Interoffice memo
C. Express forms
D. Purchase order forms
E. Employee payroll checks

Section IV—Literature Guidelines
A. Newsletter
B. Capabilities and services brochure
C. General use folder
D. Employee handbook
E. Report cover/folder

Section V—Technical Supplement Guidelines
A. Master artwork
  1. Logo sheets

Optional—
Future Sections (not included in budget)
Section VI—Special Applications Guidelines
A. Invitation card and envelope
B. Identity tags
C. Employee five-year pins
D. Audio-visual
E. Giveaways and merchandising Aids

Section VII—Advertising Guidelines
(to be developed in coordination with current advertising agency)
A. Newspaper advertisements
B. Magazines (consumer)
C. Magazines (trade)
D. Direct mail
E. Poster(s)

Section VIII—Signs
A. Exterior
B. Interior
C. Directional
D. Decals
E. Portable exhibits and displays

Work session

At a point when we have a mock-up, including the text, we will meet with you to review the manual in detail. Based on approval of the mock-up, we will then proceed to Phase III. You will be billed separately for any refinements to the manual, in content or style, after approval of Phase II work session.

PHASE II—MANUAL PRODUCTION

Based upon approval and completed revisions of the comprehensive manual mock-up, we will produce one master manual, in one color (i.e. manual mechanicals), for duplication and submission to a printer of your choice. Printing supervision and coordination are not included in the proposal. These services are available upon request.

NOTES

1. William A. Greer, "Lite Lit and Other Sines of the Times," *New York Times,* August 24, 1986.

2. Nancy Giges, "Coke's Switch a Classic," *Advertising Age,* July 15, 1985: p. 82.

3. Gordon Lippincott and Walter P. Margulies, *From Abex to Xerox* (New York: Lippincott & Margulies, 1974) p. 52.

4. "Hibernia Bank's Campaign Lures 8,000 New Customers," *San Francisco Chronicle,* July 19, 1985.

5. *Webster's New World Dictionary of the American Language* (New York: Simon and Schuster *College Edition,* 1968) p. 397.

6. Donald K. White, "Crocker Bank's Image Change," *San Francisco Chronicle,* February 16, 1983.

BIBLIOGRAPHY

DESIGN

Capitman, Barbara Baer. *American Trademark Designs*. New York: Dover Publications, 1976.

Carter, David E. *Designing Corporate Identity Programs for Small Corporations*. New York: Art Direction Book Company, 1982.

Carter, David E. *Corporate Identity Manuals*. New York: Art Direction Book Company, 1976.

Crawford, Tad. *Legal Guide for the Visual Artist*. New York: E.P. Dutton, 1979.

Crawford, Tad, and Arie Kopelman. *Selling Your Graphic Design and Illustration*. New York: St. Martin's Press, 1981.

Delano, Frank. "Unified ID System Can Aid Perceptions." *Ad Age* (July 17, 1978): 44–45.

Delano, Frank. "Corporate Identity: An Investment Worth Protecting." *Ad Age* (January 1, 1979): 16–17.

Dreyfuss, Henry. *Symbol Sourcebook: An Authoritative Guide to International Graphic Symbols*. New York: Van Nostrand Reinhold Company, 1972.

Ellinger, Richard G. *Color Structure and Design*. New York: Van Nostrand Reinhold Company, 1963.

Favre, Jean-Paul, and Andre November. *Color and Communication*. New York: Hastings House, 1979.

Flanagan, George A. *Modern Institutional Advertising*. New York: McGraw-Hill Book Company, 1967.

Gorb, Peter. *Living By Design*. New York: Watson-Guptill Publications, 1977.

Graphic Artists Guild. *Pricing and Ethical Guidelines*. New York: Graphic Artists Guild, 1985.

Holden, Donald. *Art Career Guide*. New York: Watson-Guptill Publications, 1961.

Holmes, Nigel. *Designing Pictorial Symbols*. New York: Watson-Guptill Publications, 1985.

Hurlburt, Allen. *The Design Concept*. New York: Watson-Guptill Publications, 1981.

Lippincott, Gordon, and Walter P. Margulies, *From Abex to Xerox*. New York: Lippincott and Margulies, 1974.

Margulies, Walter P. "Animals Going Out as Corporate Symbols." *Ad Age* (November 7, 1977): 60.

Marquis, Harold H. *The Changing Corporate Image*. New York: American Management Association, 1970.

Marshall Editions. *Color*. New York: The Viking Press, 1980.

Muller-Brockmann, Josef. *The Graphic Artist*

and His Design Problems. New York: Hastings House, 1961.

Ogilvy, David. Ogilvy on Advertising. New York: Vintage Books, 1985.

Pilditch, James. Communication by Design. New York, McGraw-Hill Book Company, 1970.

Rand, Paul. Thoughts on Design. New York: Van Nostrand Reinhold Company, 1971.

Rosen, Ben. The Corporate Search for Visual Identity. New York: Van Nostrand Reinhold Company, 1970.

Schutte, Thomas F. The Uneasy Coalition: Design in Corporate America. Philadelphia: University of Pennsylvania Press, 1975.

Selame, Elinor and Joe. Developing a Corporate Identity: How to Stand Out in the Crowd. New York: Lebhar-Friedman, 1977.

Stockton, James. Designer's Guide to Color. San Francisco: Chronicle Books, 1984.

Wildbur, Peter. International Trademark Design: A Handbook of Marks of Identity. New York: Van Nostrand Reinhold Company, 1979.

Wong, Wucius. Principles of Two-Dimensional Design. New York: Van Nostrand Reinhold Company, 1972.

MARKETING

Chase, Cochrane, and Kenneth L. Barasch. Marketing Problem Solver. Radnor, PA: Chilton Book Company, 1973.

Dible, Donald M. Ed. What Everyone Should Know about Patents, Trademarks, and Copyrights. Reston, VA: Reston Publishing, 1981.

Peters, Thomas J and Robert H. Waterman. In Search of Excellence. New York: Warner Books, 1982.

Ries, Al and Jack Trout. Positioning: The Battle for Your Mind. New York: McGraw-Hill Book Company, 1981.

Stern, Walter. Handbook of Package Design Research. New York: John Wiley & Sons, 1981.

CREATIVITY

Adams, James. Conceptual Blockbusting: A Guide to Better Ideas. New York: W. W. Norton & Company, 1974.

Collier, Graham. Art and the Creative Consciousness. Englewood Cliffs, NJ: Prentice-Hall Inc., 1972.

deBono, Edward. New Think. New York: Avon Books, 1967.

Elffers, Joost. Tangram: The Ancient Chinese Shapes Game. New York: Penguin Books, 1976.

Osborn, Alex. Applied Imagination. New York: Charles Scribner's Sons, 1953.

Parry, Jay A. and Kurt Hanks. Wake Up Your Creative Genius. Los Altos, CA: William Kaufmann Inc., 1983.

Von Oech, Roger. A Whack on the Side of the Head. Menlo Park, CA: Creative Think, 1983.

PSYCHOLOGY

Freud, Sigmund. An Outline of Psycho-Analysis. Translated by James Strachey. London: The Hogarth Press, 1969.

Jacobi, Jolande. Complex, Archetype, Symbol in

the Psychology of C. G. Jung. New York: Pantheon Books, 1957.

James, William. *The Principles of Psychology.* New York: Dover Publications, 1950.

Jung, C. G. *Memories, Dreams and Reflections.* London: The Fontana Library Series, 1969.

Powell, James. *The Tao of Symbols.* New York: Quill Books, 1982.

Watts, Alan. *The Book: On the Taboo Against Knowing Who You Are.* New York: Macmillan, Collier Books, 1966.

INDEX